rosemary hill

elements of style

Knit + Crochet Jewelry with Wire, Fiber, Felt + Beads

INTERWEAVE.
interweavebooks.com

This book is dedicated to my family, whom I love more than could ever be put into words.

editor katrina loving

cover and interior design pamela norman

photography annette slade
except for the following pages by rosemary hill:
15, 21, 31, 39, 43, 55, 99, 111, and 117.

photo styling connie poole

technical editors kristen tendyke
and jamie hogsett

technical illustration ann swanson

production design katherine jackson

Text © 2008 Rosemary Hill
Illustrations © 2008 Interweave Press LLC
All rights reserved.

Interweave Press LLC
201 East Fourth Street
Loveland, CO 80537-5655 USA
interweavebooks.com

Printed in China by Asia Pacific Offset

Library of Congress Cataloging-in-Publication Data
Hill, Rosemary, 1965–
Elements of style : creating jewelry with wire, fiber,
felt, and beads /
Rosemary Hill, author.
   p. cm.
Includes index.
ISBN 978-1-59668-079-1 (pbk.)
1. Jewelry making. I. Title.
TT212.H54 2008
745.594'2--dc22
        2008008683

10 9 8 7 6 5 4 3 2 1

acknowledgments

I have met so many wonderful people, without whom this book would not have been written. There are three women who particularly inspired me to think of new possibilities: Jaime Dixon (aka Scout), Terri Shea, and Cheryl Oberle. Without you three, I would not be sitting here at this moment writing this sentence. My next giant thank you must go to Amy R. Singer, the mastermind behind Knitty.com, who published my first pattern (wire and bead Venezia napkin rings). And I owe a very special debt of gratitude to my dear friend Susan Mall, whose incredible kindness and support I will never forget. A loving thank you to my boys and my husband, who have put up with me and my acres of yarn, fiber, wire, and beads. The bits and pieces of this book spent some time taking over not just my life, but the dining table, living room, office, bedroom, bathrooms, and the lives of my family as well. You have been so patient with me!

I had the incredible good fortune to work with Interweave on this book, and sometimes, I truly need to pinch myself to believe how fabulous my editors have been. Thank you so much, Tricia and Katrina! You made this process not only smooth for a first-time author, but also enjoyable. And here is where it becomes really difficult. There are so many people to thank that I couldn't possibly mention you all by name. But I hope you all know who you are (especially you, Saturday morning ladies) and understand how much I appreciate you. I am so grateful for you, my friends who have stood by me, supported me, believed in me, and let me know that you were there. I won't ever forget.

contents

Elements of Style *is a synthesis of three lifelong passions of mine: beading, knitting, and crochet.*

Life has taken me in many directions: music, marketing, graphic design, and illustration to name a few. Somehow, though, it all led back here, where it began.

Color and texture have always entranced me. I remember my mother telling me that, as a baby, I would trace the grain patterns in the wood with my finger and "talk" to them as she held me in her old rocking chair. My fascination continued when my grandmother taught me to crochet (I was in preschool at the time), and later when my mother taught me to knit. Around this time, I also became irrevocably addicted to beads and beading. I remember that, when I was eight, I received my first jewelry commission from a coworker of my mother's.

In the following pages, I hope to share my passions and stretch your imagination with a slightly different look at the art of adornment and the elements of style. What is jewelry? What classifies a piece as jewelry? What forms can it take? From what materials can it be made?

When I set about designing projects for this book, I had one umbrella concept in mind: creating pieces from beads, wire, and fiber that are wearable in many different settings, from a cocktail party to the office to a casual weekend lunch date. I used beading, crocheting, knitting, felting, and wire-working techniques freely in many different combinations to realize these designs. There's a good chance you will find mixtures of materials and techniques that you have not seen before.

The projects in this book come in all sizes and levels of difficulty, using myriad materials and techniques. You will love the tips and tricks, as well as taking old standby techniques and applying them in different ways, in different combinations, and with different materials. In the end, you will have unique pieces of jewelry that will have people asking to take a closer look.

As I write this, both my grandmother and my mother live only in the memories of those who knew them. Both had a lifelong dream of writing a book; neither ever did. It seems fitting that my first book should be dedicated to a synthesis and an exploration of the arts I learned from them.

— *Rosemary Hill*

wire

Knitting with wire was my first foray into making jewelry with needles and hooks. It was natural, loving needle arts and beading as I do, that the two should cross paths at some point. Even though I had worked extensively with wire, it was still surprising to me how simple it is to create a beautiful piece from wire and beads with knitting needles or a crochet hook. I went on to create projects that I hope you will enjoy from an aesthetic standpoint while you experiment with some techniques that may be new to you. These beautiful, sophisticated pieces are as enjoyable to create as they are to wear.

sterling frame bracelet

I love sterling silver! I love the color, the springy quality and malleability of the wire, and the beautiful way it shines up into a glowing masterpiece after looking dingy and gray. With all this in mind, I knew there would come a time when I would no longer be satisfied working with craft wire. And of course, I was right. I swatched, I designed, I swatched some more. And then, I took that irrevocable leap. I ordered a spool of 30-gauge sterling silver wire, and this bracelet was born.

materials

* 10' (9.5 m) of 30-gauge sterling silver wire

* 5 sterling silver 18x22mm rectangular links with granulated texture

* 15" (20.5 cm) of 16-gauge sterling silver wire

* 5 sterling silver 24-gauge 3" (75 mm) head pins

* 5 faceted 5x8mm mixed semiprecious stone rondelles (shown: amethyst, amazonite, red agate, olive jade, lapis lazuli)

* 5 clear ½" (12 mm) plastic 2-hole buttons

* 21 sterling silver 5x8mm figure-eight connectors

* 1 sterling silver 25mm curved bar-shaped bead

* 1 sterling silver 22mm round link with granulated texture

needles

* Size 2 (2.75 mm) bamboo dpns. (See tip on p. 20.)

tools

* Flush or side cutters; nylon-jaw pliers; steel bench block; ball peen hammer; round-nose pliers; flat-nose pliers.

gauge

* Exact gauge is not critical.

finished size

* 7½" (20 cm).

need to know

Abbreviations p. 118
Knitting Basics pp. 118–119
Lark's Head Knot p. 119
Backward-Loop CO p. 119
Garter Stitch (grtr st) p. 120
Opening and Closing a Jump Ring p. 123

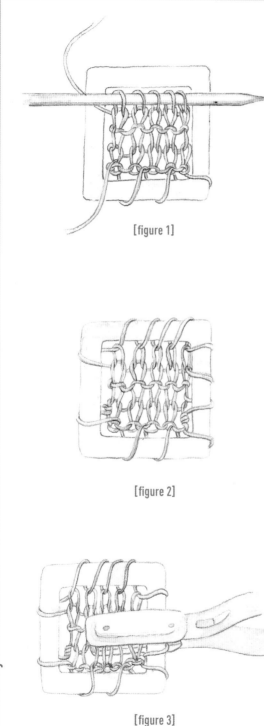

[figure 1]

[figure 2]

[figure 3]

note Throughout the pattern, the sterling silver 18x22mm rectangular links will be referred to as frames to avoid confusion with other links.

bracelet
framed knits *(make 5)*

1. Using 30-gauge wire and leaving a 4" (10 cm) tail, CO 5 sts as follows: begin with a lark's head knot and CO 3 sts using the backward-loop CO method.

2. Work 4 rows in grtr st and cut the wire using flush cutters, leaving a 5" (13 cm) tail. Straighten out the stitches gently on the needle. Do not BO.

3. Using the wire tail from the CO edge, wrap the bottom of knitted piece onto the sterling frame by passing the wire tail through a stitch each time you wrap it around the frame [figure 1]. Continue wrapping across the bottom and then up the next side until about ½" (2 cm) of wire remains. Twist the wire around a strand in the knitted piece and trim with flush cutters.

4. Using the tail of wire from the live stitches, repeat Step 3 to wrap the live stitches and the remaining side of the knitted piece to frame. Continue wrapping until all 4 sides of the knitted piece are securely attached to the frame, then wrap the wire around the knitted strand and trim using flush cutters [figure 2].

5. Using nylon-jaw pliers, flatten the stitches against the frame [figure 3]. This will ensure that there are no sharp ends of wire protruding.

figure-eight links *(make 4)*

6. Use flush cutters to cut 2" (5 cm) of 16-gauge wire (if you are trying to conserve wire, do not cut the wire before shaping). Use nylon-jaw pliers to pull the wire straight. Grasping the very end of the wire between the fattest part of the round-nose pliers, bend the wire around the pliers [figure 4].

7. With the fattest part of your pliers, grasp the longer end of the wire close to the completed loop and wrap the wire around the pliers in the opposite direction from the first wrap, forming a figure-eight shape [figure 5]. Trim the wire [figure 6].

8. Hammer one side of the link on the bench block using a ball peen hammer. The hammered side will be the back side.

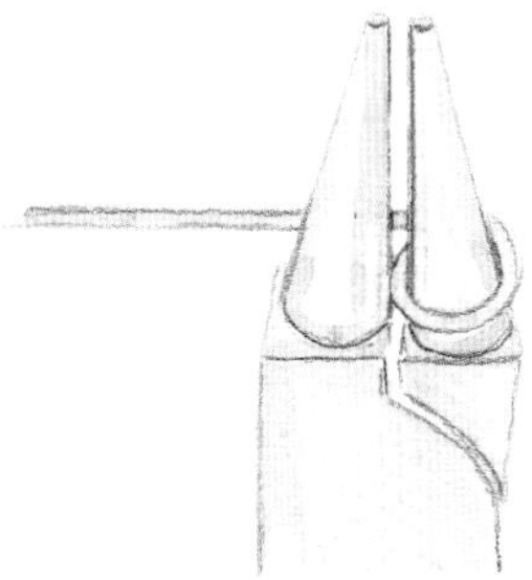

[figure 4]

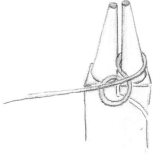

[figure 5]

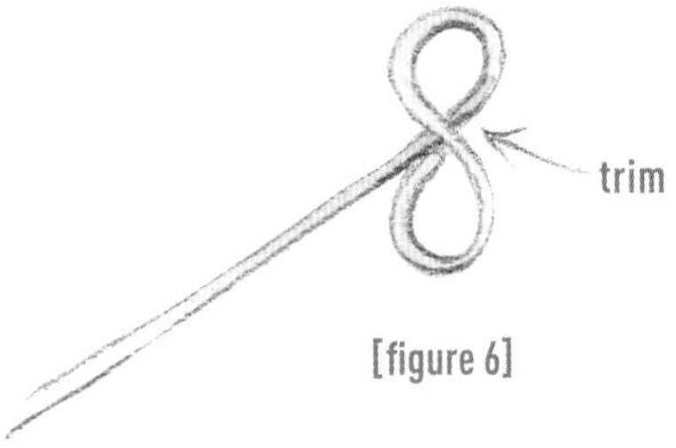

trim

[figure 6]

tips

* Open and close the premade figure-eight connectors as you would a jump ring (see p. 123). Do not simply pull the ends apart as this will distort the shape and weaken the wire.

* Practice creating a link or two of this bracelet with craft wire before you use the sterling silver wire, and practice with craft wire all the way through to attaching the knitted portions to the links. You will be glad you did! This will allow you to get used to working with wire before using the more expensive stuff.

* When attaching premade figure-eight connectors to links, use round-nose pliers if you need to in-crease the size of the hole between the knitting and the link. Gently enlarge the area. Do not push hard.

toggle bar side *2-to-1 Link*

9. Repeat Step 6 using 3" (7.5 cm) of 16-gauge wire.

10. With the middle part of your round-nose pliers, grasp the longer end of wire a little above the completed loop and wrap the wire halfway around pliers in the opposite direction from the first wrap [figure 7].

11. With the fattest part of your pliers, grasp the longer end of wire across from the completed loop and wrap the wire around the pliers toward the first loop; trim the wire [figure 8].

12. Put one end of the pliers into each loop and pull them toward each other [figure 9].

13. Hammer one side of the link on the bench block using a ball peen hammer. The hammered side will be the back side.

toggle ring side *2-to-1 Link*

14. Repeat Step 6 using 4" (10 cm) of 16-gauge wire.

15. Repeat Step 7. Do not trim the wire.

16. Using flat-nose pliers, grasp the wire where it would have been trimmed for a figure-eight connector. Turn the wire at a right angle to the connector [figure 10].

[figure 7]

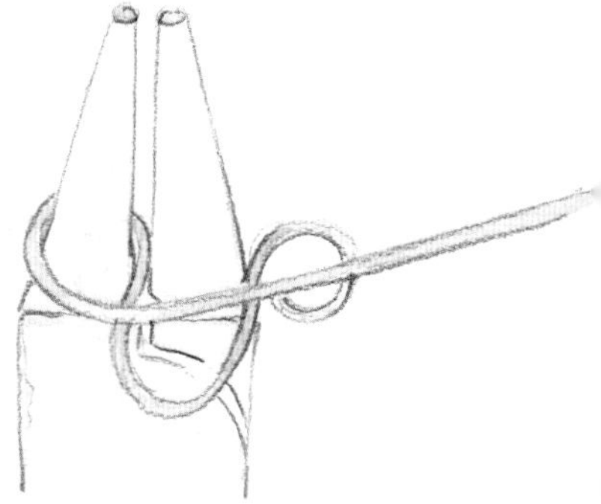

[figure 8]

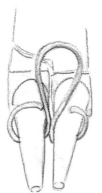

[figure 9]

[figure 10]

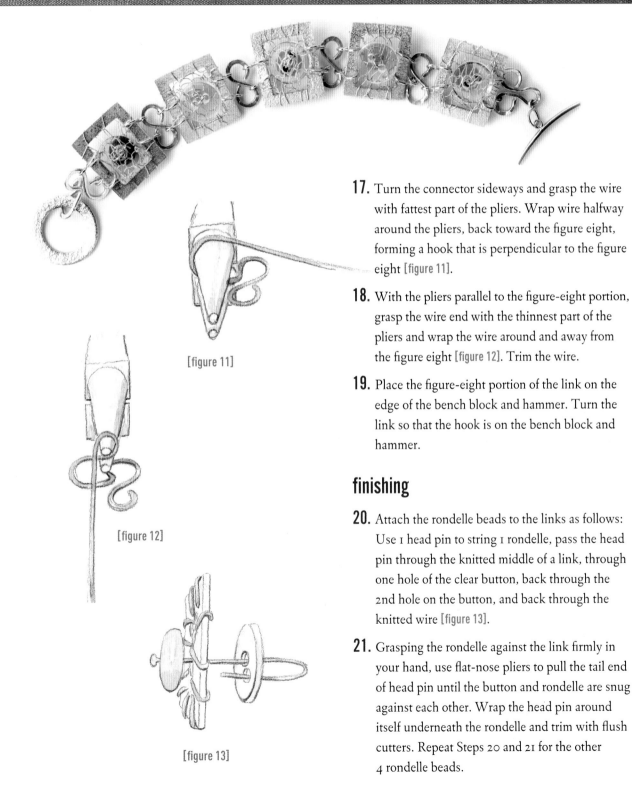

[figure 11]

[figure 12]

[figure 13]

17. Turn the connector sideways and grasp the wire with fattest part of the pliers. Wrap wire halfway around the pliers, back toward the figure eight, forming a hook that is perpendicular to the figure eight [figure 11].

18. With the pliers parallel to the figure-eight portion, grasp the wire end with the thinnest part of the pliers and wrap the wire around and away from the figure eight [figure 12]. Trim the wire.

19. Place the figure-eight portion of the link on the edge of the bench block and hammer. Turn the link so that the hook is on the bench block and hammer.

finishing

20. Attach the rondelle beads to the links as follows: Use 1 head pin to string 1 rondelle, pass the head pin through the knitted middle of a link, through one hole of the clear button, back through the 2nd hole on the button, and back through the knitted wire [figure 13].

21. Grasping the rondelle against the link firmly in your hand, use flat-nose pliers to pull the tail end of head pin until the button and rondelle are snug against each other. Wrap the head pin around itself underneath the rondelle and trim with flush cutters. Repeat Steps 20 and 21 for the other 4 rondelle beads.

[figure 14]

assembly

Assemble as follows, using premade 5×8mm figure-eight connectors to attach all links. Refer to [figure 14] for assistance with order of elements.

22. Use 1 figure-eight connector to attach the bar half of the clasp to the Toggle Bar Side 2-to-1 Link.

23. Use 2 figure-eight connectors to attach the Toggle Bar Side 2-to-1 Link to the frame with the lapis lazuli rondelle. Use 2 figure-eight connectors to attach the other side of the frame to 1 large figure-eight link.

24. Use 2 figure-eight connectors to attach the large figure-eight link to the frame with the olive jade rondelle.

25. Use 2 figure-eight connectors to attach the other side of the frame to 1 large figure-eight link.

26. Use 2 figure-eight connectors to attach the large figure-eight link to the frame with the red agate rondelle.

27. Use 2 figure-eight connectors to attach the other side of the frame to 1 large figure-eight link.

28. Use 2 figure-eight connectors to attach the large figure-eight link to the frame with the amazonite rondelle.

29. Use 2 figure-eight connectors to attach the frame to 1 large figure-eight link.

30. Use 2 figure-eight connectors to attach the large figure-eight link to the frame with the amethyst rondelle.

31. Use 2 figure-eight connectors to attach the frame to the Toggle Ring Side 2-to-1 Link. Attach the hook on the Toggle Ring Side 2-to-1 Link to the 22mm round link.

making your own findings

Often the only things separating mediocre jewelry from extraordinary jewelry are the findings: the clasp, the connectors, the chain, the jump rings, and so on.

If you have held back from making your own findings (as I did for years), thinking that it is too difficult or time-consuming, I hope you will revisit that option now! Although you can usually find suitable premade findings, many findings, like the ones used in the Sterling Frame Bracelet, are simple to make and look fantastic!

If you have not worked with wire before or made findings, I suggest practicing with a 16-gauge plated or copper craft wire to get the hang of shaping wire with pliers. This is also a good option for practicing hammering techniques to achieve textured effects.

neofiligree in copper necklace & earrings

When I first experimented with wire knitting and crochet, I realized I could make my own beads by forming wire around a knitting needle. I loved the result! There was a fluid look to the stitch pattern that brought to mind a sort of free-form filigree. This design is based on that idea. Although the materials are very traditional—copper, pearls, tigereye—the shapes and random arrangement of the elements combine to produce a piece that seems to be, at once, both classic and modern.

materials

* 1 spool (15 yd [13.8 m]) natural copper 28-gauge wire (one spool is sufficient for both necklace and earrings)

NECKLACE

* 4 copper 4x6mm oval jump rings
* 1 copper-plated (lead-free pewter) 25mm hammered toggle clasp
* 23" (58.5 cm) of copper .014 Soft Flex Metallics fine beading wire (nylon-coated stainless steel)
* 2 copper wire guardians
* 2 copper 2mm crimp tubes
* 54 copper-plated size 11° seed beads
* 46 dark brown 6mm wood rounds
* 19 copper-plated 5mm hexagonal rondelles
* 4 tigereye 10x14mm faceted rectangles
* 5 peach 28–30mm Biwa pearl sticks (drilled lengthwise)

EARRINGS

* 2 copper 2" (50 mm) head pins
* 4 copper-plated 5mm hexagonal rondelles
* 4 dark brown 6mm wood rounds
* 2 copper 4x6mm oval jump rings
* 1 pair copper-plated earring wires

needles

* Size 2 (2.75 mm) bamboo dpns (for knitting wire beads).
* Size 6 (4 mm) aluminum straight (for forming wire beads).

tools

* Flush or side cutters; nylon-jaw pliers; crimping pliers; round-nose pliers; chain-nose pliers; scissors.

gauge

* 6 stitches and 5 rows (one bead) = about ¾ x ⅞" (2 x 2.2 cm).

finished size

* Necklace: 29½" (75.5 cm).
* Earrings (including ear wires): 2¼" (5.5 cm).

need to know

Abbreviations p. 118
Knitting Basics pp. 118–119
Garter Stitch (grtr st) p. 120
Lark's Head Knot p. 119
Backward-Loop CO p. 119
Whipstitch p. 123
Finger Blocking p. 120
Opening and Closing a Jump Ring p. 123
Crimping p. 124
Stringing p. 123
Wrapped Loop p. 124

necklace
wire beads *(make 9)*

1. Leaving a 4–5" (10–13 cm) tail, with size 2 needles and copper wire, CO 6 sts as follows: begin with a lark's head knot and CO 4 sts using the backward-loop CO method.

2. Work 5 rows of grtr st. BO, cut the wire using flush cutters leaving at least a 5" (13 cm) tail.

3. Using the wire tail, whipstitch BO edge to strengthen the edge. Leave a wire tail.

4. Using the tail left when casting on, whipstitch CO edge to strengthen. Trim this wire tail.

5. Grasp the CO edge with the fingers of one hand and BO the edge with fingers of the other hand. Pull the piece to lengthen and finger block.

6. Wrap the wire piece lengthwise around the size 4 aluminum needle [figure 1] and, using the wire tail still attached to the piece, whipstitch the seam along the edges to make a cylinder. Trim the wire.

7. Using nylon-jaw pliers, apply pressure evenly around the cylinder to round the sides of the bead and mold to the needle.

8. Antique the wire beads to match the findings and other beads, using the patina technique (see p. 21).

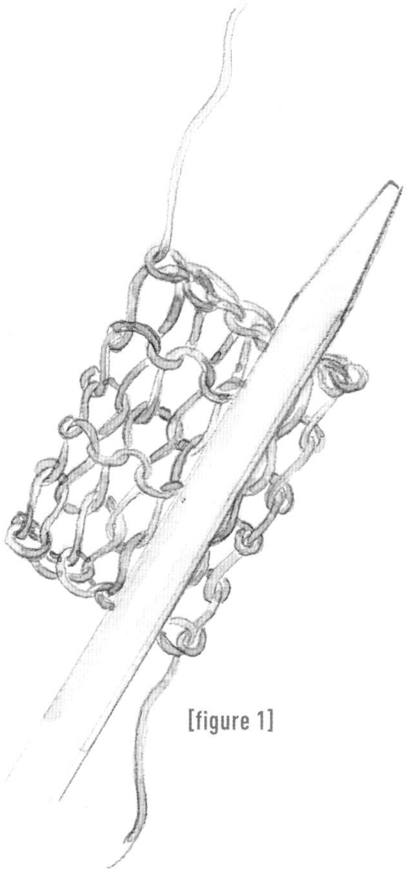

[figure 1]

assemble necklace

9. Open 1 jump ring and string 1 jump ring and the ring half of the clasp before closing (this forms a small extension for the clasp). Repeat using 2 more jump rings and the bar half of the clasp.

10. Use the beading wire to string 1 crimp tube and 1 wire guardian. Pass the beading wire back through the tube and several beads, then use crimping pliers to crimp the tube. Use a jump ring to string the wire guardian just used and the ring half of the clasp. Trim the wire.

11. Use beading wire to string 5 seed beads, 1 wood round, 3 seed beads, 3 wood rounds, 1 seed bead, 1 rondelle, 1 seed bead, 1 pearl, 3 seed beads, 1 wood round, 1 rondelle, 1 wood round, 1 wire bead, 1 wood round, 1 rondelle, 1 wood round, 3 seed beads, 1 tigereye rectangle, 1 seed bead, 1 rondelle, 1 seed bead, 1 wood round, 1 rondelle, 1 wood round, 1 wire bead, 1 wood round, 1 rondelle, 1 wood round, 1 wire bead, 1 wood round, 1 rondelle, 1 wood round, 3 seed beads, 1 pearl, 1 seed bead, 3 wood rounds, 3 seed beads, 1 wood round, 1 rondelle, 1 wood round, 1 seed bead, 1 tigereye rectangle, 3 seed beads, 1 wood round, 1 rondelle, 1 wood round, 1 wire bead, 1 wood round, 1 rondelle, 1 wood round, 1 seed bead, 1 pearl, 3 seed beads, 1 wood round, 1 seed bead, 1 wood round, 1 rondelle, 1 wood round, 1 wire bead, 1 wood round, 1 rondelle, 1 wood round, 1 wire bead, 1 wood round, 1 rondelle, 1 wood round, 3 seed beads, 1 tigereye rectangle, 1 seed bead, 1 wood round, 1 rondelle, 1 wood round, 1 wire bead, 1 wood round, 1 rondelle, 1 wood round, 3 seed beads, 1 pearl, 3 seed beads, 1 wood round, 1 rondelle, 1 wood round, 3 seed beads, 3 wood rounds, 1 wire bead, 1 wood round, 1 rondelle, 1 wood round, 1 seed bead, 1 pearl, 3 seed beads, 1 wood round, 1 rondelle, 1 wood round, 1 wire bead, 1 wood round, 1 rondelle, 1 wood round, 1 seed bead, 1 tigereye rectangle, 1 seed bead, 1 wood round, 1 seed bead, 1 crimp tube, and 1 wire guardian. Pass beading wire back through the tube and several beads and crimp the tube. Trim the wire.

earrings
wire beads *(make 2)*

1. Follow Steps 1–8 of necklace.

assemble earrings

2. Use 1 head pin to string 1 rondelle, 1 wood round, 1 wire bead, 1 wood round, and 1 rondelle. Form a wrapped loop.

3. Use 1 jump ring to connect the wrapped loop and 1 ear wire.

4. Repeat Steps 2 and 3 to make the second earring.

* It is usually best to use bamboo needles when knitting with wire because they are less slippery than metal needles, thus making it easier to work with the wire. You will probably want to devote a set of needles solely to working with wire as it will eventually score the surface of the bamboo.

patinas

If you have ever seen a bronze statue with a greenish coating where it has weathered, you have seen a patina. Patina is caused by the reaction of a metal to chemicals on its exposed surfaces. Although there are many colors of patina that can be achieved by the application of chemicals, an "antique" patina will result naturally from a metal's chemical reaction to the elements over time. But what to do when you want the look of age without the wait? Apply your own!

I antiqued (oxidized) the copper wire beads in this project to match the findings using something most of you probably have in your kitchen right now—eggs! This technique allowed me to get the same effect as I would have gotten by using liver of sulfur, but without having to buy or handle chemicals.

The entire process can take between 30 minutes and two days, depending on the result you wish to achieve. I started with three hard-boiled eggs (6-minute eggs, but boiling them longer is fine) and crushed them, shell and all. I broke up the yolk quite a bit to ensure that the chemicals therein would be distributed as much as possible.

I placed the eggs and beads in a ziplock bag and sealed it. It sat on the counter for a day, and I turned the beads over several times to make sure the copper oxidized evenly. When I was happy with the result, I removed the beads and washed them thoroughly. And that's all there was to it!

I had a small "knitting doll" as a child, and I spent hours playing with it. I remembered it so fondly that when I saw the little Wonder Knitter sitting on a shelf at my local yarn store, I absolutely had to have it! Secretly, I was imagining painless feet of I-cord for felted bags, but in reality, it sat patiently in its packaging waiting for the right time to shine. Enter wire knitting! As soon as I threaded my little toy and knit a few rounds, I knew I had hit on something! And after a fair amount of tweaking and playing, this necklace was born.

materials

* Smooth cotton waste yarn
* 3 spools (72 yd [44 m]) silver-tone 34-gauge wire
* 64" (162.5 cm) of .014 Soft Flex fine beading wire (nylon-coated stainless steel)
* 2 silver-plated 6mm cord caps
* 22 apple coral 12mm round beads
* 4 silver-plated 2x3mm crimp tubes
* 2 silver-plated wire guardians
* 2 silver-plated 4mm round beads
* 1 apple coral 39mm "GoGo" pendant
* 3 silver-tone 5mm jump rings
* 1 silver-plated (lead-free pewter) 18mm toggle clasp

tools

* Knitting doll or other mechanical knitter with 6-peg capability; flush or side cutters; round-nose pliers; chain-nose pliers; scissors.

gauge

* Exact gauge is not critical.

finished size

* 22" (56 cm).

need to know

Knitting Doll p. 121
Abbreviations p. 118
Knitting Basics pp. 118–119
Slipknot p. 121

necklace
knitted tubing (make 2)

1. Using a knitting doll with 6 pegs, thread the cotton waste yarn and work 2 rnds.

2. Switch to doubled 34-gauge wire. Mark the beginning of the round by placing a small piece of tape near the first peg on the knitting doll. Do not tie knots! Be sure to leave a tail of about 4" (10 cm).

3. After working 2 rnds, thread the CO tail of wire through the center of the knitting doll (from top to bottom) and pull gently to lengthen, being careful not to pull it closed; guide the knitted tubing through the center.

4. Work a total of 35 rows in wire, pushing and pulling the wire tubing gently through the aperture.

5. Remove the tubing from the knitting doll and run a piece of waste yarn through the live stitches to keep them from raveling. Trim the wire with flush cutters, leaving a 5" (12.5 cm) tail.

add beads

6. Remove the waste yarn from the CO edge of tubing, run the wire tail through the live stitches, secure, and pull tight. Fold about ¼" (6 mm) of the tubing back onto itself; this end will be placed in a cord cap in Step 8.

7. Use 16" (40.5 cm) of beading wire to string the wire tubing, beginning with the open end and being careful not to catch any stitches. Pass the beading wire through the end of the tubing where it has been folded over.

8. String 1 cord cap, one 4mm round, and 1 crimp tube. Pass the beading wire through 1 wire guardian. Pass back through the crimp tube, 4mm bead, and cord cap [figure 1]. Make sure the beading wire is snug through the wire guardian and flatten the crimp tube using chain-nose pliers.

9. Push the folded end of the tubing gently into the cord cap, making sure the wire tubing is firmly lodged inside [figure 2].

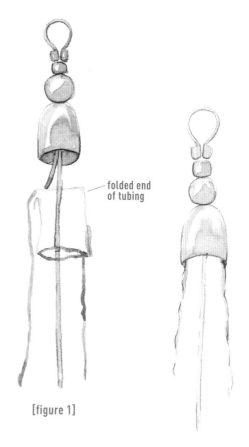

folded end of tubing

[figure 1]

[figure 2]

[figure 3]

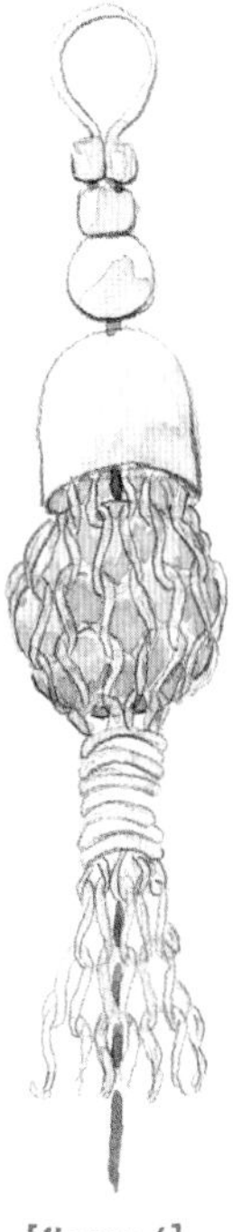

[figure 4]

10. Use the beading wire to string eleven 12mm round beads and carefully push them into the tube. Pull the waste yarn on the end of the tube to tighten and tie it using a slipknot to prevent the beads from slipping off the beading wire.

11. Push the first bead up against the cord cap and stretch and mold the wire tubing tightly around the bead [figure 3].

12. Insert one end of a 12" (30.5 cm) piece of 34-gauge wire through the bead (toward the cord cap) to secure. Wrap the other end of the wire tightly around the tubing under the 12mm round bead for about ¼" (6 mm). Wrap back toward the bead and back down again, so that the bead becomes completely stationary [figure 4]. Pass the end of the wire through the wraps to conceal and secure.

13. Repeat Steps 11 and 12 nine times. There should be 1 bead and about 3" (7.5 cm) of tubing remaining. If there is more tubing than needed, it will be unraveled in Step 15 on p. 26.

tips

* When attaching findings to knitted and crocheted wire jewelry, it is important to avoid putting too much stress on the fine-gauge wire, which will cause wire fatigue and premature breakage. In this piece, I have used beading line to bear the weight of the beads, which will help protect the more delicate wire tube from wear and tear. The beading line is attached to both the clasp and the pendant, thereby strengthening the piece considerably.

* Wire must be pulled gently through the knitting doll. I used a combination of methods: both pushing through with my finger and pulling the wire gently through from the opposite side to keep the tube open but moving through the aperture.

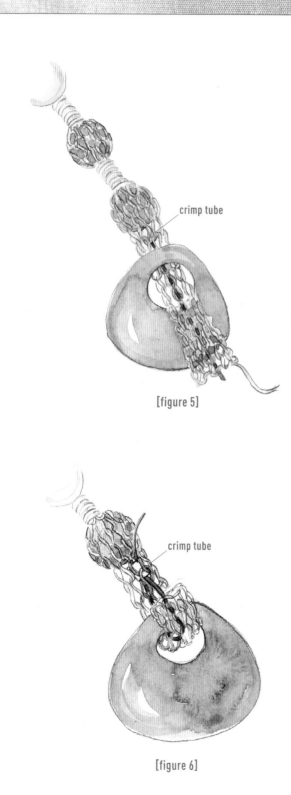

[figure 5]

[figure 6]

crimp tube

crimp tube

attach pendant

14. Push the last bead up against the wrapping after the previous bead. Use the beading wire to string 1 crimp tube and snug it up against the bead. Flatten the remaining tubing and pass it (with the beading wire) through the pendant [figure 5]. Wrap the end of the tubing around the pendant so that the end of the tubing comes to the space between the last bead and the pendant.

15. Remove the waste yarn and run the ends of the wire through the live stitches to secure. If there is too much remaining tubing to fit in the space between the last bead and the pendant, ravel a few rows carefully until it fits properly and then thread the wire ends through the live stitches to secure. The beading line will still be protruding from the end of the tubing.

16. Use the beading wire to weave through the tubing in order to pass the beading wire back through the crimp tube [figure 6] and the eleventh bead. If necessary, adjust the placement of the pendant so that the area between the last bead and the pendant is about ½" (1.3 cm).

17. Use chain-nose pliers to flatten the crimp tube. Use flush cutters to trim the beading wire. Fold the tubing into place against itself, between the eleventh bead and the pendant and mold it into a thick tubular shape. Repeat Step 12, wrapping the wire around the double thickness of wire tubing and making sure you conceal the crimp tube [figure 7].

18. Use the second piece of knitted tubing to repeat Steps 6–17 for the other side of the necklace.

19. Use 1 jump ring to attach the ring half of the toggle clasp to 1 wire guardian at one end of the necklace. Use a chain of 2 jump rings to attach the bar half of the clasp to the other wire guardian at the other end of the necklace.

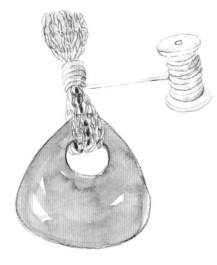

[figure 7]

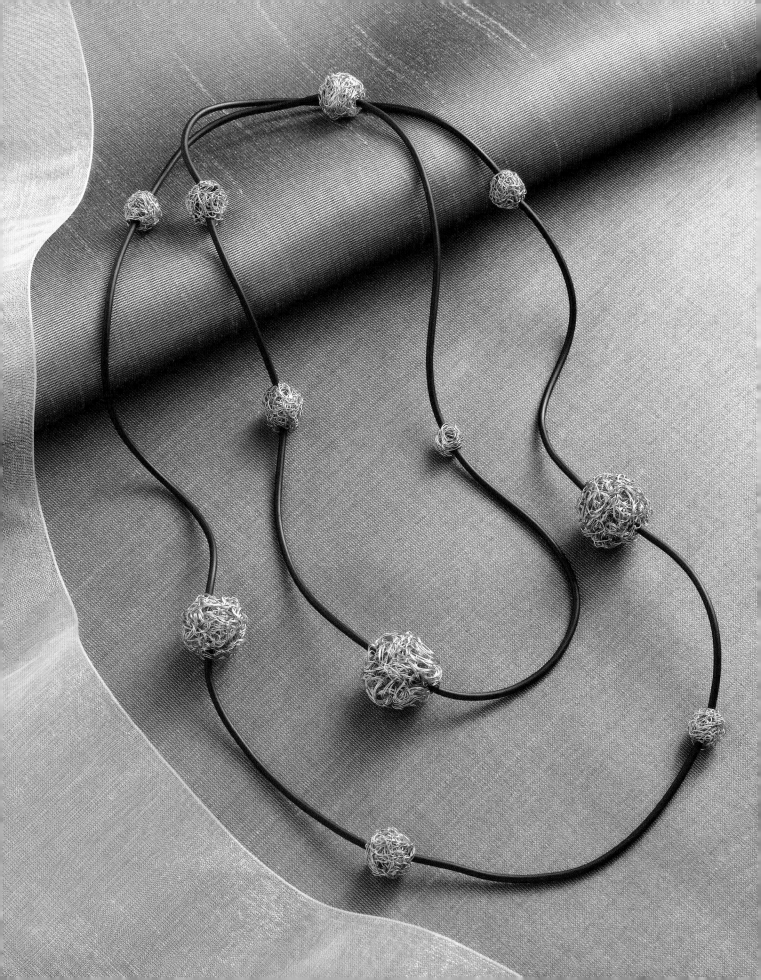

Knitting with wire takes some getting used to. I have knit swatch after swatch after swatch, all in the great quest for the best needles and wire combinations. Although I am a fairly tight knitter with yarn, I learned to loosen up quite a bit when working with wire, lest I suffer the painful consequences of an overly tight grip! But what to do with all of those swatches? Enter the Mess-up Necklace, a perfect resting place for all of my swatches. And as a bonus, I got to crush, mangle, and crumple all of those unworthy bits of wire that had refused to cooperate!

materials
* A collection of knit and/or crochet wire swatches
* 45" (114.5 cm) of 2mm black rubber (neoprene) cord
* Wire of same color and gauge as swatches for stabilizing swatch balls (I used silver-tone 34-gauge craft wire)

tools
* Round-nose and/or chain-nose pliers; metal awl (fairly heavy weight); flush or side cutters; scissors.

finished size
* 39" (99 cm).

need to know
Stringing p. 123
Square Knot p. 118

necklace

1. Roll the wire swatches into balls in the palms of your hands. They will be of varying sizes. I used 11 swatches for this piece (and I confess that I made some of them just for this necklace).

2. When the swatches have been formed into balls, poke holes through the center with the metal awl. Grasp the ball firmly and work the awl through the center, twisting and applying firm pressure.

3. String the balls onto the rubber cord and arrange as desired, making sure either to begin or to the end with a larger ball. This ball will hide the knot in the rubber cord.

4. Tie the ends of the rubber together, using a square knot. Pull tight and trim the ends.

5. Move the swatch ball over the top of knot and press the ball with your fingers around the knot to encase it entirely in the swatch ball.

6. The other balls will still slip easily up and down the rubber so that they can be arranged. When you are happy with placement of the balls, press the balls to the cord so that they are stationary on the cord.

7. You will now stabilize the swatch balls. Thread wire that is the same color as your swatches through each ball, catching stitches and weaving the wire in and out of the ball until the ball stays tightly together and does not slip up and down the cord. Wrap the wire around itself several times and trim. Use round- or chain-nose pliers to aid in working with the wire if necessary and/or to flatten wire ends against the swatch. Be gentle to avoid crushing the swatch balls. Tuck any wire ends inside the balls.

wire hardness

Ever wonder what it means when your wire is labeled with a specific hardness, such as "dead soft" or "half hard"? Read on for an explanation of the different degrees of hardness. Now you will know exactly what to look for, and why!

"Dead soft" refers to wire that has been annealed, a process that strengthens and reduces brittleness by heating and then slowly cooling the metal. This makes the wire very easy to bend and work. Dead-soft wire is the most appropriate for knitting and crochet, but be aware that the wire needs to be carefully worked; the less you bend it back and forth, the less likely you are to fatigue the wire and leave it vulnerable to breakage.

"Half-hard" wire is less malleable than dead-soft wire but is still soft enough to be relatively easy to manipulate. Half-hard wire is most commonly used for wire-wrapped projects.

"Full-hard" wire is the least malleable of the three and is not easily manipulated.

donut break necklace & earrings

This one is all about color!

When I first designed this necklace, I intended to use rough sponge coral donuts. But it wasn't meant to be. When I was ready to begin, those rough sponge coral donuts became unavailable. Back to the drawing board. First I looked for horn or bone. Then I looked for wood. Finally, I stumbled upon resin. I absolutely could not resist it; the colors were amazing! I began to search for resin donuts and soon hit the jackpot when I found Judy of Natural Touch Beads! And oh! The colors! Racks and racks of the most beautiful, glowing colors imaginable. I wanted it all. But . . . practicality ruled the day, and this is what I came away with!

materials
* 2 spools (48 yd [43.9 m]) of Artistic Wire silver non-tarnish 34-gauge silver-plated copper wire
* waste yarn (optional)

NECKLACE
* 16 resin 32mm flat donuts in the following colors: 4 cobalt; 3 capri; 1 clear; 4 artichoke; 4 light blue
* 304 gunmetal 6mm jump rings
* 52 silver 6mm jump rings
* 3 yd (2.7 m) gunmetal 4mm chain

EARRINGS
* 2 cobalt resin 31x23mm teardrop slices
* 4 gunmetal 6mm jump rings
* 2 silver 6mm jump rings
* 1 pair gunmetal ear wires

needles
* Size 2 (2.75 mm) bamboo dpns. (See Tip on p. 21.)

tools
* Flush or side cutters; flat-nose and/or chain-nose pliers; nylon-jaw pliers.

gauge
* Exact gauge is not critical.

finished size
* Necklace: 57" (1.4 m).
* Earrings (including ear wires): 2½" (6 cm).

need to know
Abbreviations p. 118
Knitting Basics pp. 118–119
Garter Stitch (grtr st) p. 120
Lark's Head Knot p. 119
Backward-Loop CO p. 119
Whipstitch p. 123
Opening and Closing a Jump Ring p. 123

necklace
wire wraps for resin donuts
(wrap 16 donuts)

1. With wire doubled and dpns, leaving a 4" (10 cm) wire tail, CO 5 sts as follows: begin with a lark's head knot and CO 3 sts using the backward-loop CO method.

2. Work 10 rows in grtr st. Cut wire with flush cutters, leaving a tail of at least 4" (10 cm). Leave stitches live on needle.

3. With wire CO tail, whipstitch CO edge, stopping at the middle of the knitted piece.

4. Thread the knitted piece through a resin donut [figure 1] and wrap around.

5. Run CO tail through the hole in the resin donut from the outside to the center, through the stitches of the knitted piece [figure 2]. Do not trim.

6. Remove the needle from the live stitches (you can insert a piece of waste yarn through the stitches to hold them in place if you wish) and, with wire attached to live stitches, whipstitch live stitches to CO edge and trim.

7. Flatten the wire together over the resin donut using chain-nose pliers [figure 3].

8. Run CO tail back through the hole in the resin donut from the center to outside, catching a stitch on the inside of the resin donut to hold the wire in place.

9. Weave CO tail in and out of stitches to the edge, then wrap the wire around edge to strengthen.

10. With chain-nose pliers, poke two holes through the ends of the stitches above the resin donut [figure 4].

11. Repeat Steps 1–10 to create a wire wrap for the other side of the same resin donut.

12. Repeat Steps 1–11 for each resin donut, until each has 2 wire wraps (you should have 32 total wire wraps).

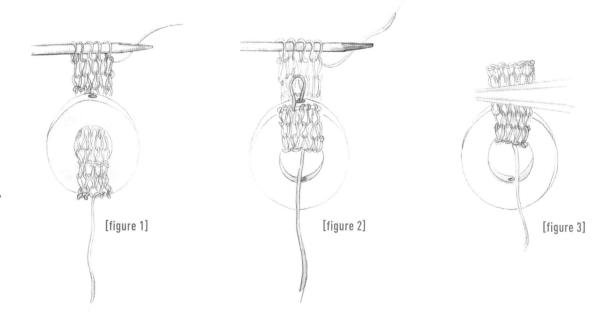

[figure 1] [figure 2] [figure 3]

wire segments *(make 9)*

13. With wire doubled and dpns, CO 5 sts as follows: begin with a lark's head knot and CO 3 sts using the backward-loop CO method.

14. Work 5 rows in grtr st and BO all sts.

15. Whipstitch along CO edge with the wire tail to strengthen.

16. Whipstitch along BO edge with the wire tail to strengthen.

17. With chain-nose pliers, poke one hole in each corner (as in Step 10).

[figure 4]

jump ring segments *(make 26)*

See [figure 5] for assistance with instructions below.

18. Using flat-nose and chain-nose pliers (or two of either kind) attach 1 gunmetal jump ring to 2 gunmetal jump rings. Attach 1 more gunmetal jump ring to the 2 jump rings so that you have two pairs of rings.

19. Repeat Step 18, attaching 2 silver jump rings to the previous 2 jump rings.

20. Repeat Step 18, attaching 2 gunmetal jump rings to the previous 2 jump rings. Repeat Step 18 again using gumetal jump rings.

21. Repeat Steps 18–20 twenty-five times (you should have 26 jump ring segments).

[figure 5]

chain segments

22. Cut gunmetal chain into eight 1¼" (3.2 cm) and sixteen 1" (2.5 cm) pieces (you will have a total of 24 pieces).

assembling necklace

Read through entire step before continuing.

23. The necklace is assembled using four different types of segments to connect the resin donuts. The following gives assembly instructions for each segment type. Skip to Assembly Order on p. 37 for instructions on how each segment will be used before creating any of the segments below.

SEGMENT A: Use 2 gunmetal jump rings to attach one hole of a wire wrap on 1 donut to one end of a chain segment. Use 2 gunmetal jump rings to attach the other end of the 1" (2.5 cm) chain segment to one hole of one wire segment. Use 2 gunmetal jump rings to attach the other end of the wire segment to one end of a second 1" (2.5 cm) chain segment. Use 2 gunmetal jump rings to attach the opposite end of the 1" (2.5 cm) chain (2.5 cm) segment to one hole of a wire wrap on a second donut. Repeat all to connect the other holes of the wire wraps on the donuts and wire segment.

SEGMENT B: Attach the 2 gunmetal jump rings on one end of a jump ring segment to one hole of the wire wrap on 1 donut. Attach the 2 gunmetal jump rings on the opposite end of the jump ring segment to one hole of a wire segment. Attach the 2 gunmetal jump rings on one end of a second jump ring segment to the opposite end of the wire segment. Attach the 2 gunmetal jump rings on the opposite end of the second jump ring segment to one hole of a wire wrap on a second

[segment a]

[segment b]

[segment c]

[segment d]

donut. Repeat all to connect the other holes of the wire wraps on the donuts and wire segment.

SEGMENT C: Use 2 gunmetal jump rings to attach one hole of a wire wrap on 1 donut to one end of a 1¼" (3.2 cm) chain segment. Use 2 gunmetal jump rings to attach the opposite end of the 1¼" (3.2 cm) chain segment to one hole of a wire wrap on a second donut. Repeat all to connect the other holes of the wire wraps on the donuts.

SEGMENT D: Attach the 2 gunmetal jump rings on one end of a jump ring segment to one hole of a wire wrap on 1 donut. Attach the 2 gunmetal jump rings on the other end of the jump ring segment to one hole of a wire wrap on a second donut. Repeat all to connect the other holes of the wire wraps on the donuts.

ASSEMBLY ORDER: Use the following order to attach the resin donuts using the segment types listed. Refer back to the previous segment instructions to assemble each type.

Clear resin donut, segment A, cobalt resin donut, segment B, capri resin donut, segment C, light blue resin donut, segment B, artichoke resin donut, segment A, capri resin donut, segment D, light blue resin donut, segment C, cobalt resin donut, segment B, artichoke resin donut, segment C, light blue resin donut, segment B, cobalt resin donut, segment A, artichoke resin donut, segment D, capri resin donut, segment A, cobalt resin donut, segment B, light blue resin donut, segment C, artichoke donut, and segment D that attaches to the other side of the clear resin donut.

earrings
wire wraps *(make 2)*

1. With wire doubled and dpns, CO 3 sts as follows: begin with a lark's head knot and CO 1 st using the backward-loop CO method.

> **ROW 1:** Knit.
> **ROW 2:** Yo, k across row—4 sts.
> **ROW 3:** Yo, k across row—5 sts.

finishing

2. Continue working straight for 10 rows in grtr st. Cut wire, leaving a tail of at least 4" (10 cm). Leave sts live on needle.

3. Thread the knitted piece through a teardrop slice [figure 1] and wrap around.

4. Remove the needle from the live stitches (you can insert a piece of waste yarn through the stitches to hold them in place if you wish) and using wire attached to live stitches, whipstitch to middle of knitted piece, leaving tapered end free [figure 2].

5. Thread the wire through the hole in the top of the teardrop slice from the outside to the center, through one or more stitches of the knitted wire wrap, and back through the hole in the teardrop slice from the center to the outside. Wrap the wire around the stitches (as in Step 9 on p. 34) to hold tight and secure.

6. With CO tail, wrap the wire around the middle stitch in top of the earring several times to reinforce the piece [figure 3]. This also creates a small hole. Trim the wire.

7. Flatten the wire with chain-nose pliers above teardrop slice. You may also need to shape the top of the wire wrap so that it tapers properly. This can easily be done by hand with the malleable wire.

8. Attach 2 gunmetal jump rings to the hole in the knitted wire at the top of the earring. Use 1 silver jump ring to attach 1 ear wire to the 2 gunmetal jump rings.

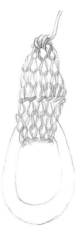

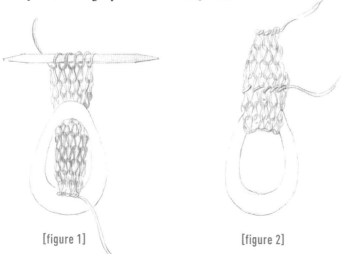

[figure 1]   [figure 2]   [figure 3]

what is resin?

Natural resins, such as amber, come from plants, and start life as a viscous substance that hardens over time. Natural resins are generally clear to dark brown in color but can sometimes be found in other colors, such as green and even blue.

Synthetic resins are man-made materials similar in composition and behavior to natural resins; they are viscous materials capable of hardening. Synthetic resins are put to numerous uses, such as epoxies,

varnishes, cements, statuary, furniture, and, of course, beads! The resin beads used in this piece come from a cottage industry in Java, Indonesia, and were designed by and made for Natural Touch Beads in Petaluma, California. They have the look of a beautiful frosty piece of sea glass but without the weight or fragile nature of glass! They are wonderfully light and colorful, but remember to buy enough for your project. As with many handmade items, the colors change subtly with each batch made.

trio of wire earrings

[rose quartz triangles]

[wire rounds]

Instant gratification!

My favorite kind of project. This
trio of earrings starts with a simple
project and gets more challenging
with each pair. If you work them in
order, my bet is that you will be a
master when you finish.

[beaded rectangles]

beaded rectangles

knit rectangles *(make 2)*

1. CO 9 sts as follows: begin with a lark's head knot and CO 7 sts using the backward-loop CO method.

2. Work 10 rows in grtr st, finger blocking as you go. BO and trim wire, leaving a 12" (30.5 cm) tail.

add beads

3. You will now be beading the edges of the rectangles (use both the CO and the BO tails). *Use the tail wire to string 1 bead and whipstitch around the edge of the knit rectangle [figure 1]; repeat from * until you are satisfied with the arrangement of beads, making sure that both sides (front and back) of the wire edges are covered.

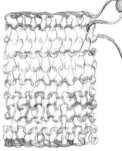

[figure 1]

4. Insert the hook closure through top center stitch of the knitted piece (under the beads). Use chain-nose pliers to bend the hook enough to prevent the knitted piece from slipping out [figure 2]. Use 1 jump ring to connect the hole of the hook to 1 ear wire.

5. Repeat Steps 3 and 4 for the second earring.

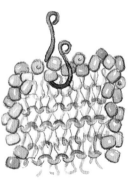

[figure 2]

note
Depending on how dense you would like the beads to be, you may run out of wire. If this happens, cut a new length of wire and wrap it around the edge of the knit rectangle several times, as close as possible to the last bead. When you string the next bead, position it over the wire wrap and secure tightly to hide the beginning of the new wire.

materials
* 1 spool (24 yd [22 m]) of silver-tone 34-gauge wire
* About 200 emerald green rainbow matte size 8° seed beads
* 2 gunmetal hook clasps
* 2 gunmetal 5mm jump rings
* 1 pair gunmetal ear wires

needles
* Size 2 (2.75 mm) bamboo dpns. (See tip on p. 20.)

tools
* Chain-nose pliers; flush or side cutters.

gauge
* Exact gauge is not critical.

finished size
* Including ear wires: 1¼" (3.2 cm) wide x 2½" (6.5 cm) long.
* Knitted portion only: about 1" (2.5 cm) wide x 1½" (4 cm) long.

need to know
Abbreviations p. 118
Knitting Basics pp. 118–119
Lark's Head Knot p. 119
Backward-Loop CO p. 119
Garter Stitch (grtr st) p. 120
Finger Blocking p. 120
Whipstitch p. 123

wire rounds earrings
rounds

Make 2 circles in each color as follows:
With hook and wire, ch 5, join with sl st.

RND 1: Sc 16 in ring, join with sl st—16 sc.

RND 2: Ch 1, *sc 1, sc 2 in next st, repeat from * to end of rnd, join with sl st—24 sc.

RND 3: Ch 2, *dc 2, dc 2 in next stitch, repeat from * to end of rnd, join with sl st—36 dc.

Fasten off. Weave in wire, wrap around a stitch to secure, and trim with flush cutters.

assembly

1. Open 1 jump ring and string 1 chartreuse round and 1 blue round, through the last row of stitches at the outside edge of each round before closing the jump ring.

2. Attach 1 ear wire to the last row of stitches on the outside edge of the chartreuse round, directly across from the jump ring. If you find it difficult to get the ear wire through the wire round, use chain- and/or round-nose pliers to gently open the ring of the ear wire as you would a jump ring; string the wire round, and close the ring of the ear wire.

3. Repeat Steps 1–2 for the other earring so that the second earring is in opposite color orientation to the first.

materials
* 32-gauge Artistic Wire silver-plated copper wire; 1 spool each in blue and chartreuse
* 2 silver-plated 5mm jump rings
* 1 pair silver-plated ear wires

hook
* Size 5 (1.7 mm) steel.

tools
* Round-nose or chain-nose pliers; flush or side cutters.

gauge
* Exact gauge is not critical.

finished size
* Including ear wires: 2¾" (7 cm).
* Wire rounds: 1" (2.5 cm) in diameter.

need to know
Abbreviations p. 118
Crochet Basics pp. 121–122
Double Crochet (dc) p. 122
Opening and Closing a Jump Ring p. 123

tip

* When you are assembling these earrings, if you find it difficult to slip the wire rounds onto the jump ring or earring wire, you can use a small metal awl to gently enlarge a stitch hole in the wire round.

working with different types of wire

Are all wires created equal? In a word, no. But with a little patience and practice, you can become master of them all. Let's explore three commonly used types of wire: sterling silver, silver-toned copper, and silver-plated copper.

The least expensive of these is the silver-toned copper wire. This is a great wire to use when trying new ideas and perfecting your technique. It is easy to work with and so affordable that you won't care about using a ton of it for swatches (which you will fashion into several Mess-up Necklaces on p. 28, anyway, right?). Once you feel comfortable working with the wire, you may want to move on to one of the other types, as the silver-toned copper wire doesn't always match other silver findings in color.

Next up on the affordability scale are silver-plated wires. Some manufacturers also make these in different colors, including Artistic Wire's chartreuse, my personal favorite! The plain silver-plated wire will match the color of most silver-plated findings, and because the core of the wire is malleable copper, it is still very easy to work with.

Finally, there is sterling silver wire, the most expensive of the three. If you have practiced ahead of time with other craft wire, you will be well prepared to work with the sterling silver wire. It is also important to be aware of the different levels of hardness wire comes in, especially if you plan to knit or crochet the wire (see p. 31).

materials
* 20" (51 cm) of Rings & Things silver-plated 18-gauge craft wire
* 6 rose quartz 6x7–9mm tumbled beads
* 1 coil (82' [25 m]) of Rings & Things silver-plated 32-gauge craft wire
* 1 pair silver-plated ear wires

needles
* Size 0 (2 mm) metal dpns.

tools
* Flush or side cutters; felt pen; flat-nose pliers; nylon-jaw pliers; chain-nose pliers; round-nose pliers.

gauge
* Exact gauge is not critical.

finished size
* Including ear wires: 1⅛" (3 cm) at widest point x 3" (7.5 cm) long.

need to know
Abbreviations p. 118
Knitting Basics pp. 118–119
Garter Stitch (grtr st) p. 120
Simple Loop p. 124
Finger Blocking p. 120
Opening and Closing a Jump Ring p. 123

rose quartz triangles
triangle frames *(make 2)*

1. Cut 10" (25.5 cm) of 18-gauge wire and use the felt pen to mark a spot 3½" (9 cm) from one end. Use flat-nose pliers to bend the wire at the mark at about a 105° angle, as shown in [figure 1]. Use the long end of the wire to string 3 rose quartz beads.

2. Use flat-nose pliers to bend the longer end of wire up next to the rose quartz nuggets, at the same angle as the first wire, forming a triangle.

[figure 1]

3. Measure 2" (5 cm) from the bend formed in Step 1 and use flat-nose pliers to bend the wire so that the tail is parallel to the base of the triangle [figure 2].

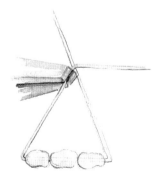

[figure 2]

4. Measure 2" (5 cm) from the bend formed in Step 2 and use flat-nose pliers to bend the wire tail so that it points straight up and is perpendicular to the base of the triangle.

5. Adjust the wire tails so that the bends meet and use nylon-jaw pliers to grip the triangle immediately below the intersection. Use chain-nose pliers to wrap the parallel wire around the perpendicular wire, forming a wrap with three coils [figure 3]. Trim the parallel wire, but do not trim the perpendicular wire.

Use round-nose pliers to form a simple loop with the perpendicular wire on top of the coils formed in Step 5. Trim the wire.

6. Repeat Steps 1–5 for the other triangle, making a mirror image of the first triangle.

cast on to triangle

7. Wrap 32-gauge wire around the right leg of the triangle frame at the base [figure 4]. With dpns, CO 6 stitches around rose quartz nuggets in the manner indicated in Steps 8–10 (be sure to keep the tip of the working needle close to the stitches so that wire can easily pass over needle):

8. With the needle and wire in front of the triangle, wrap the wire from front to back around the needle, under the base of the triangle between the 1st and 2nd beads, and up around the needle from back to front [figure 5].

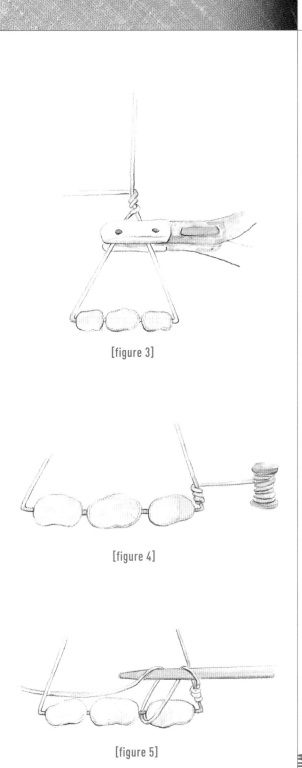

[figure 3]

[figure 4]

[figure 5]

9. Bring the wire through to the back between the needle and the triangle base and wrap under the base of the triangle, between the 1st and 2nd beads, and up between the needle and the triangle base to wrap the needle with another stitch from back to front. Bring the wire under the triangle base and wrap another stitch over the needle from back to front (4 sts CO, [figure 6]).

10. Wrap the wire under the triangle base from back to front, between the 2nd and 3rd beads, and around the needle from front to back; then pass the wire between the needle and the triangle base to the front. Wrap the wire under the triangle base between the 2nd and 3rd beads and pass the wire between the needle and the triangle base to the front. Wrap the wire around the needle from front to back, under the triangle base, between the 2nd and 3rd beads, and up around the needle from front to back. Bring the wire behind the left leg of the triangle so that it will be anchored around this leg when the work is turned (6 stitches cast on, [figure 7]).

knitting in triangle

11. Turn work; make sure that the needle holding the stitches is behind the wire triangle and the working wire is in front. Insert working needle through the triangle and through the stitch to knit; make sure that the working wire is brought around the triangle leg from front to back so that wire is anchored around the edge of the triangle [figure 8].

12. Complete the row across, knitting as for the first stitch.

13. Turn work; continue in grtr st for 13 more rows, finger blocking after each row (with work on needles). Make sure that the needle holding the stitches is always behind the wire triangle and the working wire goes around the outside of triangle each time you turn the work.

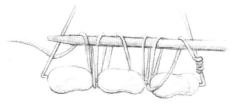

[figure 7]

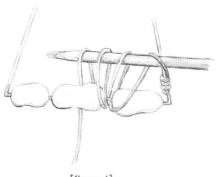

[figure 6]

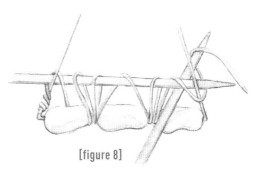

[figure 8]

tips

* Make sure you choose rose quartz nuggets or equivalent beads that enable you to make equal sized triangles.

* Because the 32-gauge wire is packaged in a coil, I first wrapped it onto a spool and then put it in a small plastic bag to keep it from unravelling as I worked.

* Metal knitting needles are used because of their greater strength in the smaller sizes. Try to find needles with a less slick texture, such as Inox brand Pearl Grey double-pointed knitting needles (see Resources, p. 126).

14. Cut the wire, leaving a 5″ (13 cm) tail. Thread the tail around outside the triangle and back through the live stitches.

15. Pull the wire tight and wrap several times around the top of the wire triangle (under the existing wire wrap from the legs of the triangle), back down, through at least one stitch of the last row and back up. Wrap several more times around the previous wrap and trim. Tuck the wire tail in and crush it flat with nylon-jaw pliers against the wraps.

16. Repeat Steps 7–15 for the other earring. Work the second earring in opposite direction from first earring to create a mirror image (you will have 2 sts anchored between the 1st and 2nd beads, the 3rd and transitional st anchored on one side between the 1st and 2nd beads and on the other side between the 2nd and 3rd beads, and 3 sts anchored between the 2nd and 3rd beads [with the last of these sts also being anchored around the leg of the triangle].

assembly

17. Use chain-nose pliers to open 1 ear wire as you would a jump ring and attach it to the wrapped loop formed in Step 5. Repeat for the second earring.

fiber

The projects in this section did not come to me immediately, but once the ideas began to flow, wonderful things happened. The first image that popped into my head was of a scarf . . . or was it a necklace? Really it was both: a delicate scarflike necklace. The next day, I drove to a yarn store that stocks Habu Textiles yarns, because I knew immediately that it had to be made of one of the most fascinating materials that I have ever come across: Habu's laceweight silk and stainless steel yarn. From there, the projects branched out, using linen, hemp, and a multitude of lovely beads and findings. I hope you will enjoy these as much as I do!

This amazing stainless steel and silk yarn from Habu Textiles is the most unusual yarn I have ever used. It is soft and lovely, but the stainless steel core holds a shape like fine wire. When I went about designing this project, I knew it needed to be something that would take advantage of the characteristics of the material, soft and flowing, while still retaining the elegance and delicacy of a lovely piece of jewelry. And then it came to me: an organically shaped scarf necklace that can easily be draped around the neckline of your little black dress.

materials

YARN

Laceweight (#0 Lace) stainless steel blend *Shown:* Habu Textiles A-20 1/20 silk/stainless steel (69% silk, 31% stainless steel; 622 yd [560 m]/1 oz [28 g]): #3 gray, about 311 yd (284.3 m [or ½ oz]).

* 425 (8 g) iridescent gray size 11° hex seed beads

* 25 crystal cal 1x 4mm crystal bicone beads

* 25 silver shade 4mm crystal bicone beads

* About 6" (16 cm) of scrap 32–34-gauge wire

needles

* Size 0 (2 mm), size 2 (2.75 mm), and size 6 (4 mm) bamboo dpns.

notions

* Big Eye beading needle; tapestry needle; fray-stop or sewing needle and thread (optional).

gauge

* 40 sts and 38 rows = 4" (10 cm) in st st on smaller needles. Exact gauge is not critical.

finished size

* 2½" (6.5 cm) at widest point x 72" (183 cm) long.

need to know

scarf necklace
prepare beads

1. With Big Eye beading needle and yarn, string about 360 seed beads.

first end section

2. With yarn and size 6 needles, CO 25 sts using the cable CO method, placing a seed bead after each.

ROW 1 (RS): Knit.

ROW 2: Purl.

ROW 3: Switch to size 2 needles, and work in st st, dec 1 st at both edges of row as follows: ssk, work to last 2 sts, k2tog—23 sts rem.

ROW 4: Purl.

ROW 5: Switch to size 0 needles, and work in st st, dec 1 st at both edges of row as in Row 3—21 sts rem.

3. Work in st st until piece measures 4½" (11.5 cm), at the same time, work 3 Short-Row Ruffles (see special stitches below) on each edge, spaced according to your taste, then dec 1 st at both edges of every knit row (every other row) 5 times—11 sts rem.

4. (RS) Knit 1 row, placing a seed bead after each st.

5. (WS) Purl 1 row.

note

Each end section has about 61 seed beads and 2 or 3 crystals. There are 4 or 5 eyelets and 6 short-row sequences. While working this section, place seed beads (see Tips at right), crystals, short-row sequences, and eyelets according to your taste. There are 21 middle sections. Each middle petal section has 10–14 seed beads and 1–3 crystals arranged randomly according to your taste. Each middle "petal" section has 2–4 eyelets, and uses 3 or 4 short-row sequences to create additional ruffles in the edge of the fabric.

special stitches

Eyelet

ROW 1: Work to point where eyelet is desired, yo to create extra stitch, work to end of row.

ROW 2: Work row.

ROW 3: Work to extra yo stitch, drop stitch and ravel down 2 rows, work to end of row.

Short-Row Ruffle

Working in st st:

ROW 1: Work 8 sts in st st, turn. Do not wrap.

ROW 2: Work 8 sts in st st.

ROW 3: Work 4 sts in st st, turn. Do not wrap.

ROW 4: Work 4 sts in st st.

tips

* This pattern leaves room for your interpretation of the design. It is meant to look random and organic, so keep that in mind while you are knitting! As knitted, each section of the sample scarf is different.

* Finger block constantly as you are working (while the piece is still on the needles).

* **Two methods for placing beads are used:**

  1. Pre-stringing the seed beads allows you to place them as you wish by pulling up a bead close to the needle so that it is caught in the next stitch as you knit.

  2. Placing the crystals with the wire method allows for more random placement of the crystals among the seed beads. This way you don't have to know exactly where you want them ahead of time. It also reduces wear and tear on the yarn, as the crystals have small holes and often have sharp edges that catch on the yarn when pulled back and forth, which the pre-stringing method requires.

Bend the scrap piece of wire in half to form a V shape [figure 1].

Thread one end of the wire through the last stitch on the needle until the yarn sits in the bend [figure 2].

Pull the stitch off the needle, holding with the wire, and thread a bead onto both ends of the wire. Snug the bead down over the stitch [figure 3].

Place the stitch back onto the needle and remove the wire [figure 4].

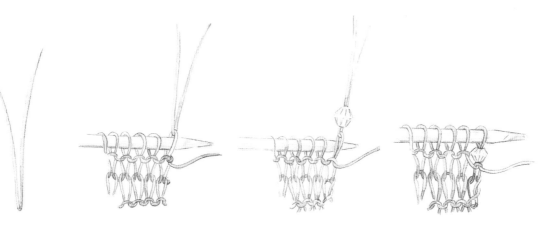

[figure 1] [figure 2] [figure 3] [figure 4]

middle petal sections

6. Begin with 11 sts on the needle from the end section. Working in st st, inc 1 st by yo at the beg of every row, excluding incomplete short rows, until section is 21 st in width. Dec 1 st by k2tog at the beg of every row, excluding incomplete rows, until section is 11 st in width. Meanwhile, use short rows to create ruffle in edge of fabric. Placement is not critical. The sample uses 3 or 4 short-row sections per petal.

7. Repeat Step 6 twenty times for a total of 21 petal sections.

8. Cut yarn, leaving an 8" (20.5 cm) tail.

second end section

9. String 65 seed beads onto yarn and work another end section as for the first end section, but do not work the last row (purl row). Cut yarn, leaving an 8" (20.5 cm) tail. Graft end section to main body of necklace using Kitchener Stitch.

10. Weave in ends using a tapestry needle and secure using fray-stop or sewing thread.

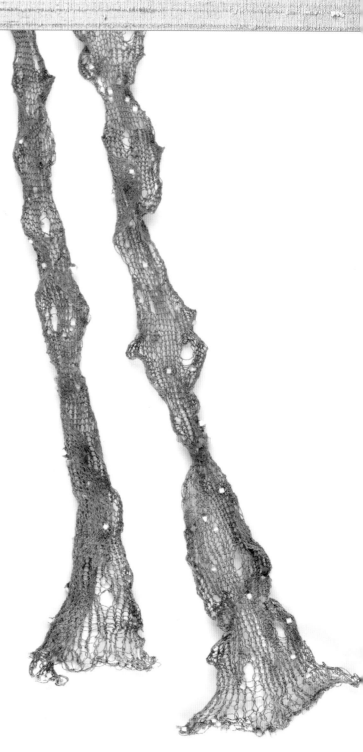

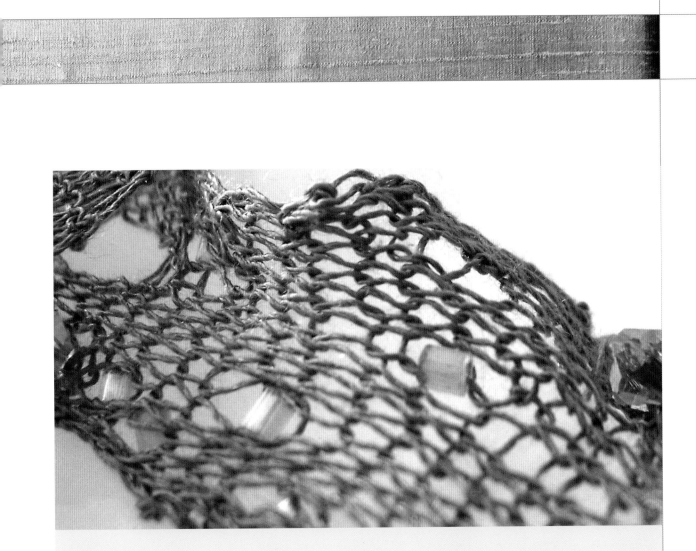

capitalizing on your materials

The unique nature of silk/stainless steel yarn is what makes this project work. It is able to hold a shape enough to use stockinette stitch without fear of the resulting fabric rolling uncontrollably. Instead, you can finger block it into lovely organic shapes.

You may be thinking: I always substitute yarns, so why is this pattern any different? Because this pattern is designed specifically to take advantage of the way this particular yarn behaves in the stitches used here. The shape achieved in this scarf necklace is unique, due to the very special characteristics of the silk/stainless steel yarn. The short rows are added to emphasize the curl and ruffle that appear in the edges. You will be delighted with the end result of using a yarn that allows you to achieve dimension in such a delicate piece.

luscious silk bracelets

Something that really intrigued me

was the effect of a single strand of this yarn knitted on small needles. It resulted in the ability to gather and ruffle, and the fabric held its shape. With the Jade Ruffle Bracelet I used a gathering technique that my mother taught me when I was a little girl. The Silk and Pearls Bracelet was molded, almost like clay, into a three-dimensional, sculptural form. Be sure to try out the beautiful earring variation as well (see p. 62)!

[silk and pearls bracelet]

[jade ruffle bracelet]

jade ruffle bracelet

wire foundation

1. With wire doubled and larger needles, CO 3 sts as follows: begin with a lark's head knot and CO 1 st using the backward-loop CO method.

ROW 1: Knit.

ROW 2: Yo, k3—4 sts.

ROW 3: Yo, k4—5 sts.

ROWS 4–51: Work in grtr st (about 5½" [14.5 cm] or 2" [5 cm] less than desired bracelet length).

ROW 52: Ssk, k3—4 sts.

ROW 53: Ssk, k2—3 sts.

ROW 54: Thread wire end through live stitches and shape end into point, then shape opposite end into point.

2. Weave in wire and wrap ends of wire around themselves to secure. Use flush cutters to trim.

larger ruffle

3. With stainless steel/silk yarn and smaller needles, CO 135 stitches using cable CO method.

4. Work 8 rows in st st, end WS row. BO all stitches and leave a 10" (25.5 cm) tail.

need to know

materials

YARN

Laceweight (#0 Lace) stainless steel blend *Shown:* Habu Textiles, A-20 1/20 silk/stainless steel (69% silk, 31% stainless steel; about 622 yd [560 m]/1oz [28 g]): #3 gray, about 50 yd (45.7 cm).

* 2 spools silver-tone 32-gauge copper craft wire (2 spools are sufficient for both bracelets; wire is used doubled)

* 21 olive jade 4mm faceted round beads

* 2 silver-plated 4x8mm prong bails

* 4 silver-plated 4mm jump rings

* 1 silver-plated (lead-free pewter) 18mm square toggle clasp

needles

* Size 0 (2 mm) metal and size 2 (2.75 mm) bamboo dpns.

tools and notions

* Flush or side cutters; flat- and/or chain-nose pliers; Big Eye beading needle; sewing needle; straight pins; contrasting color sewing thread.

gauge

* 40 sts and 38 rows = 4" (10 cm) with yarn in st st on size 0 needles.

* 5 sts and 38 rows = ½ x 5" (1.3 x 12.7 cm) in grtr st with wire doubled on size 2 needles.

* Exact gauge is not critical.

finished size

* ½ (1.3 cm) wide x 7½" (19 cm) long.

[figure 1]

smaller ruffle

5. With stainless steel/silk yarn and smaller needles, CO 135 sts using cable CO.

6. Work 6 rows in st st, end WS row. BO all sts and weave in end with sewing needle.

finishing

7. Finger block both ruffle pieces and pin them together so the edges match up (length should be about 13½" [34.5 cm]).

8. With contrasting sewing thread and sewing needle, baste ruffles together by stitching loosely down the center with smaller ruffle on top as shown in [figure 1]; do not trim thread. Holding one end of thread in one hand, gently slide knitted material along basted stitches with other hand, bunching it evenly into ruffles, until it measures about 5½" (14 cm).

9. Pin ruffles into place on wire foundation, leaving about ½" (1.3 cm) of wire exposed on either end. With BO tail and sewing needle, whipstitch ends of both ruffles into place on wire.

* Finger block ruffles gently as you knit to achieve the desired shape.

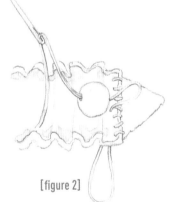

10. With working yarn, begin stitching ruffles to the wire foundation along the length of the bracelet, adding an olive jade bead on top of the smaller ruffle by passing the yarn through the bead before completing the stitch [figure 2]. Pass through all layers (ruffles and wire) and back up through layers catching wire stitches on the reverse side. Pass through the bead again, then through all layers once more, catching stitches through the ruffles and wire foundation. Add another bead in the same manner. Repeat along the length of the bracelet to add 21 beads.

11. Whipstitch the opposite ruffle edges to the wire foundation, trim, and weave in end.

12. Attach a bail to the pointed tip at one end of the wire foundation by bringing the prongs together, with about ½" (1.3 cm) at the tip of the wire in between the prongs [figure 3]. Make sure that prongs overlap when closed. Repeat with the other bail at the opposite side of the bracelet.

13. Using flat- and/or chain-nose pliers, use 1 jump ring to attach the ring half of the clasp to 1 bail.

14. Use flat- and/or chain-nose pliers to form a chain of three jump rings. Attach one of the end jump rings to the bail. Attach the other end of the jump rings to the bar half of the clasp.

[figure 2]

[figure 3]

materials

YARN

Laceweight (#0 Lace) stainless steel blend
Shown: Habu Textiles, A-20 1/20 silk stainless steel (69% silk, 31% stainless steel; 622 yd [560 m]/1 oz [28 g]): #3 gray, about 50 yd (45.1 m).

* 2 spools silver-tone 32-gauge copper craft wire (2 spools are sufficient for both bracelets; wire is used doubled)

* 48 yd (43.7 m) 34-gauge silver-tone wire

* 8 silver-plated size 11° Czech seed beads

* 70 iridescent gray size 11° Japanese seed beads

* 29 gray-blue 6mm button pearls

* 2 silver-plated 4x8mm prong bails

* 2 silver-plated jump rings

* 1 silver-plated 18mm (lead-free pewter) square toggle clasp

needles

* Size 0 (2mm) metal and size 2 (2.75 mm) bamboo dpns.

tools and notions

* Flat-nose and/or chain-nose pliers; flush or side cutters; Big Eye beading needle; sewing needle; straight pins.

gauge

* 40 sts and 38 rows = about 4" (10 cm) with yarn in st st on size 0 needles.

* 5 sts and 38 rows = about ½ x 5" (1.3 x 12.7 cm) with wire doubled on size 2 needles.

* Exact gauge is not critical.

finished size

* ½ (1.3 cm) wide x 7½" (19 cm) long.

silk and pearls bracelet
wire foundation

1. With 32-gauge wire doubled and size 2 needles, CO 3 stitches as follows: begin with a lark's head knot and CO 1 st using the backward-loop CO method.
   ROW 1: Knit.
   ROW 2: Yo, k3—4 sts.
   ROW 3: Yo, k4—5 sts.
   ROWS 4–41: Work in grtr st until piece measures 5" (12.7 cm) from beg.

2. Finger block wire gently on needle as you knit the following.
   ROW 42: Ssk, k3—4 sts.
   ROW 43: Ssk, k2—3 sts.
   ROW 44: Thread wire end through live stitches and shape end into point, then shape opposite end into point.

3. Weave in wire ends to secure. Trim using flush cutters.

knitted fabric

4. With stainless steel/silk yarn and smaller needles, CO 15 stitches as follows: begin with a lark's head knot and CO 13 sts using the backward-loop CO method.

need to know

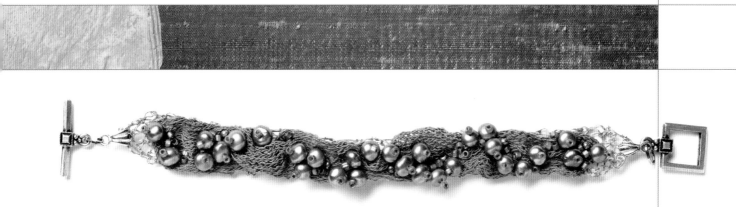

5. Work in st st for 5½" (14 cm), finger blocking material on the needles as you go.

6. BO all stitches, leaving a tail of at least 18" (46 cm).

7. Thread BO tail through sewing needle and weave in and out of BO stitches to gather edge slightly to match the shape of the wire foundation. Repeat with CO tail to gather CO stitches; do not trim.

finishing

8. Arrange knitted fabric on wire base, leaving about ⅜" (1 cm) of wire foundation at each end of knitted fabric; pin edges into place.

9. Arrange extra knitted fabric in the middle into pleasing swirls and valleys to create a three-dimensional effect; pin in place.

10. With CO tail from knitted fabric and Big Eye beading needle, begin to stitch knitted fabric to wire foundation. Add seed beads and pearls, arranging randomly, to your taste as follows:

    Pass needle up through wire foundation and knitted material and through 1 pearl and 1 seed bead. Pass back through pearl [figure 1] and then back through knitted material and wire foundation (to add seed beads alone, repeat this process without pearls).

 Many pearls have very small holes. If the yarn will not pass through the pearl a second time, you can use heavy-duty sewing thread to secure them instead.

11. Continue adding pearls and seed beads, while stitching knitted portion to wire foundation until you reach the opposite edge. Fasten off yarn and trim; weave in ends.

12. Attach a bail to the pointed tip at one end of the wire foundation by bringing the prongs together, with about ½" (1.3 cm) at tip of wire in between prongs [see figure 3 on p. 59]. Make sure that the prongs overlap when closed. Repeat with the other bail on the opposite side of the bracelet.

13. Use flat- and/or chain-nose pliers and 1 jump ring to attach the loop of 1 bail and 1 half of the clasp. Repeat with the other bail and opposite side of the toggle clasp.

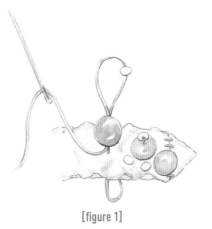

[figure 1]

materials

* In addition to the yarn and wire (left over from bracelets) listed on p. 60, you will need the following:

* 2 gray-blue 7–8mm button pearls

* 2 iridescent gray size 11° Japanese seed beads

* 2 silver-plated 3x7mm prong bails

* 1 pair silver-tone ear wires

needles, tools, and gauge

For required needles, tools, and gauge information, see p. 60.

finished size

Including ear wires: about 1½" (4.5 cm).
Wire foundation: ½" (1.3 cm) wide x 1⅛" (3 cm) long.

silk pearl earrings
wire foundation *(make 2)*

1. With wire doubled and size 2 needles, CO 5 sts as follows: begin with a lark's head knot and CO 3 sts using the backward-loop CO method.

ROWS 1–7: Work in grtr st.

ROW 8: Ssk, k1, k2tog—3 sts.

ROW 9: Knit.

ROW 10: Run wire through live stitches and shape end into point.

Weave in wire ends to secure. Trim using flush cutters.

knitted fabric *(make 2)*

2. With stainless steel/silk yarn and size 0 needles, CO 15 stitches as follows: begin with a lark's head knot and CO 13 sts using the backward-loop CO method.

ROWS 1–14: Work straight in st st, finger blocking material on the needles as you go.

3. BO all stitches, leaving a tail of at least 10" (25.5 cm).

4. Thread BO tail through sewing needle and weave in and out of BO stitches to gather slightly to match the shape of the wire foundation. Repeat with CO tail to gather CO stitches; do not trim.

finishing

5. Arrange first piece of knitted fabric on 1 wire foundation so that CO edge of fabric lines up with bottom (straight) edge of wire foundation, leaving about ⅜" (1 cm) of wire foundation exposed at pointed end.

6. Arrange extra knitted fabric in middle to desired 3-D effect and pin.

7. With CO tail from knitted fabric and Big Eye beading needle, whipstitch edge of knitted fabric to wire foundation.

8. Continue to stitch knitted fabric to wire foundation to desired effect, adding a pearl and seed bead [see Step 10 and figure 4 on p. 61] near the middle of the knitted fabric, close to the inside edge. Fasten off yarn and trim; weave in ends.

9. Attach a bail to the pointed tip at one end of one wire foundation by bringing the prongs together, with about ¼" (6 mm) at the tip of the wire in between the prongs [see figure 3 on p. 59]. Make sure that the prongs overlap when closed.

10. Using flat- and/or chain-nose pliers, open the bottom loop of 1 ear wire as you would a jump ring and attach it to the loop of the bail.

11. Repeat Steps 5–10 for the second earring, attaching the pearl so that the second earring is a mirror image of the first.

fiber earrings

I've always loved making earrings because they are so quick and yet so impressive. I may be the master of jewelry instant gratification! Here are three fun little projects. Each is simple to make and requires few materials . . . and they all turn heads!

[flowery earrings]

[gypsy earrings]

[sail earrings]

flowery earrings

knitted portion *(make 2)*

1. With silk/stainless steel yarn, CO 20 stitches as follows:
begin with a lark's head knot and CO 18 sts using the
backward-loop CO method.

2. Work 24 rows in st st, finger blocking as you work. BO
loosely and weave in ends.

finishing

3. Use 1 eye pin to string one size 6° seed bead.

4. With RS of knitted square facing, use the eye pin to pass
through the center of the knitted square from the WS to the
RS [figure 1].

5. Use the eye pin to string 1 bead cap and 1 sterling silver round
bead [figure 2]. Push the bead cap and bead down so that the
bead cap is snug over the knitted material and size 6° seed bead
(underneath the knitted material).

6. Use chain- or flat-nose and round-nose pliers to form a
wrapped loop that attaches to 1 ear wire. Trim the wire with
flush cutters.

7. Repeat Steps 3–6 for the second earring.

[figure 1]

[figure 2]

materials

YARN
Laceweight (#0 Lace) stainless steel blend
Shown: Habu Textiles, A-21 1/20 silk stainless
steel (69% silk, 31% stainless steel; 622 yd
[560 m]/1 oz [28 g]): #16 lavender, about 15
yd (13.7 m).

* 2 sterling silver 2" (50 mm) 20-gauge eye
pins

* 2 clear size 6° glass seed beads

* 2 Thai silver 8x12mm bead caps

* 2 sterling silver 2.5mm
seamless round beads

* 1 pair sterling silver ear wires

needles

* Size 0 (2mm) metal dpns.

tools

* chain-nose or flat-nose pliers; round-nose
pliers; flush or side cutters.

gauge

* 40 sts and 38 rows = 4" (10 cm) in st st
with silk/stainless steel yarn.

* Exact gauge is not critical.

finished size
Including ear wires: 2¼" (5.5 cm).

need to know

materials

YARN

Laceweight (#0 Lace) stainless steel blend
Shown: Habu Textiles, A-20 1/20 silk stainless
steel (69% silk, 31% stainless steel; 622 yd
[560 m]/1 oz [28 g]): #03 gray, 15 yd (13.7 m).

* 2 peacock 9–10mm freshwater pearls

* 2 sterling silver 2.5mm seamless
  round beads

* 2 sterling silver wire guardians

* 1 pair sterling silver ear wires

needles

* Size 0 (2mm) metal dpns.

tools

* Fine sewing needle; flush or side cutters;
  round-nose and/or chain-nose pliers.

gauge

* 40 sts and 38 rows = 4" (10 cm) in st st.

* Exact gauge is not critical.

finished size

* Including ear wires: 3¾" (9.5 cm).

need to know

sail earrings
knitted portion

Earrings are contructed to be mirror images of each other.

First earring: Leaving a tail of at least 8" (20.5 cm),
CO 15 stitches with cable CO method.

ROW 1 (RS): Knit.

ROW 2, AND ALL WS ROWS: Purl.

ROW 3 (RS): K13, k2tog—14 sts rem.

ROW 5 (RS): K12, k2tog—13 sts rem.

ROW 7 (RS): K11, k2tog—12 sts rem.

ROW 9 (RS): K10, k2tog—11 sts rem.

ROW 11 (RS): K9, k2tog—10 sts rem.

ROW 13 (RS): K8, k2tog—9 sts rem.

ROW 15 (RS): K7, k2tog—8 sts rem.

ROW 17 (RS): K6, k2tog—7 sts rem.

ROW 19 (RS): K5, k2tog—6 sts rem.

ROW 21 (RS): K4, k2tog—5 sts rem.

ROW 23 (RS): K3, k2tog—4 sts rem.

ROW 25 (RS): K2, k2tog—3 sts rem.

ROW 27 (RS): K3tog—1 st rem.

Fasten off and leave tail of at least 8" (20.5 cm).

Second earring: Leaving a tail of at least 8" (20.5 cm),
CO 15 stitches with cable CO method.

ROW 1 (WS): Purl.

ROW 2, AND ALL RS ROWS: Knit.

ROW 3 (WS): P13, ssp—14 sts rem.

ROW 5 (WS): P12, ssp—13 sts rem.

ROW 7 (WS): P11, ssp—12 sts rem.

ROW 9 (WS): P10, ssp—11 sts rem.

ROW 11 (WS): P9, ssp—10 sts rem.

ROW 13 (WS): P8, ssp—9 sts rem.

ROW 15 (WS): P7, ssp—8 sts rem.

ROW 17 (WS): P6, ssp—7 sts rem.

ROW 19 (WS): P5, ssp—6 sts rem.

ROW 21 (WS): P4, ssp—5 sts rem.

ROW 23 (WS): P3, ssp—4 sts rem.

ROW 25 (WS): P2, ssp—3 sts rem.

ROW 27 (WS): P3tog—1 st rem.

Fasten off and leave tail of at least 8" (20.5 cm).

[figure 1]   [figure 2]

finishing

1. Use the CO tail and the fine sewing needle to string 1 freshwater pearl and 1 sterling silver bead. Pass back through the freshwater pearl [figure 1].

2. Gently snug the freshwater pearl against the edge of stitches. Use CO tail to tie an overhand knot around the first side of CO tail, against freshwater pearl [figure 1]. Weave CO tail back into knitted portion, tie off, and trim with flush cutters.

3. Use the BO tail to string 1 wire guardian and 1 ear wire. Pass BO tail through the wire guardian once more [figure 2].

4. Gently snug the wire guardian to the edge of stitches, making sure the wire guardian passes through the loop of the ear wire. Use BO tail to tie an overhand knot around the first side of BO tail, snug against the wire guardian.

5. Weave BO tail back into the knitted portion, tie off, and trim.

6. Repeat Steps 1–5 for the other earring.

materials

YARN
Laceweight (#0 Lace [*14/2]) linen, cotton, or hemp
Shown: Louet North America, Euroflax 14/2 Linen (100% linen, 530 yd [484.6 m]/3.5 oz [100 g]): #35 mustard, 30 yd (27.4 m).

* 18 metallic brass size 6° Czech seed beads

* 2 plastic 1" (2.5 cm) rings

* 2 copper 4x6mm oval jump rings

* 1 pair copper ear wires

hook

* Size 4 (1.75mm) steel.

tools

* Big Eye beading needle; round-nose and/or chain-nose pliers.

gauge

* Exact gauge is not critical. Entire plastic ring needs to be covered.

finished size

* Including ear wires: 1¼ (3.2 cm) wide x 2¾" (7 cm) long.

need to know

Abbreviations **p. 118**
Crochet Basics **pp. 121–122**
Double Crochet (dc) **p. 122**
Stringing **p. 123**
Overhand Knot **p. 118**

gypsy earrings
cover rings *(make 2)*

1. Using the Big Eye beading needle and about 15 yd (13.7 m) of yarn, string 9 beads.

RND 1: Begin with a sl st on the hook and sc 70 sts around ring, or number needed to completely cover ring; sl st into first sc to join, turn.

RND 2: Ch 4 (counts as dc, ch 2), skip one sc and dc into next sc, [ch 2, skip one sc and dc into next sc] 7 times, ch 4, skip sc and sl st into next sc, turn.

RND 3: Ch 1, sl st in ch-4 sp, ch 1, sc in same sp, slide bead up, 2 sc in same sp, [sc in next ch-1 sp, slide bead up, 2 sc in same ch-1 sp] 8 times; sl st in same sp, ch 1, sl st in same sp; sl st to first rnd, fasten off and weave in ends.

finishing

2. Open 1 jump ring and thread through yarn that is looped around ring (not stitch), making sure you catch at least two strands of yarn [figure 1] and making sure you attach the jump ring on the opposite side of the ring from the fifth seed bead (so that the beads and jump ring are centered across from each other). Before closing the ring, attach the ring to 1 ear wire.

3. Repeat Step 2 for the other earring.

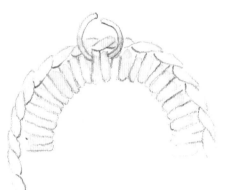

[figure 1]

* 14/2 (see Materials list at left) is the classification used by weavers for the weight of yarn featured in this project. It is equivalent to the CYCA Laceweight (#0 Lace) classification used by knitters and crocheters.

Inspiration—sometimes it's a mystery, sometimes it's obvious. And sometimes, like this time, the something that inspires us is so completely different from the result that it hardly bears mentioning. Can you believe the inspiration for this was some cream-colored leather disks? When I began experimenting with knit and crocheted pieces for this necklace, I realized how much the earthy colors of the yarn added to the overall look. But something was lacking. And then it came to me. Aqua. It was practically crying out for aqua. And then it sang to me.

materials

YARN
Laceweight (#0 Lace [14/2]) cotton, linen, or hemp
Shown: Louet North America, Euroflax 14/2 Linen (100% linen, 530 yd [484.6 m]/ 100 g cone): about 30 yd (27.4m) each in #35 mustard; #48 aqua; #62 citrus orange; #55 willow; #02 ginger; 7½ yd (6.8 m) #53 caribou.

* 136 black size 11° seed beads

* 65 reddish brown 3x6mm wood cylinder beads

* 6 copper knot cups

* 2 copper 30mm 3-to-1 connectors

* 4 copper 4x6mm jump rings

* 1 copper 16mm toggle clasp

hook

* Size 2 (2.2 mm) steel.

tools and notions

* Awl or knitting needle to assist in placement of knots; chain-nose or flat-nose pliers; flush or side cutters; small sharp-tipped tapestry needle; G-S Hypo Cement.

gauge

* Exact gauge is not critical.

finished size

* 36" (91.5 cm).

need to know

Abbreviations p. 118
Overhand Knot p. 118
Crochet Basics pp. 121–122
Stringing p. 123
Knot Cup p. 124

necklace

one-round circles *(make 7)*

Make one-round circles (about ½" [1.3 cm])—4 citrus orange, 1 mustard, 1 willow, and 1 aqua, as follows:

Ch 8; join with sl st (ring made).

RND 1: Ch 1, sc 20 in ring; join with sl st—20 sc. Fasten off and weave in ends.

two-round circles *(make 12)*

Make two-round circles (about ¾" [2 cm])—5 aqua, 1 willow, 1 mustard, and 5 ginger, as follows:

Ch 5; join with sl st (ring made).

RND 1: Ch 1, sc 12 in ring; join with sl st—12 sc.

RND 2: Ch 1, *sc 2 in first st, sc; repeat from * to end of rnd; join with sl st—18 sc. Fasten off and weave in ends.

three-round circles *(make 6)*

Make three-round circles (about 1" [2.5 cm]) —3 willow and 3 mustard, as follows:

Ch 5; join with sl st (ring made).

RND 1: Ch 1, sc 12 in ring; join with sl st—12 sc.

RND 2: Ch 1, *sc 2 in first st, sc; repeat from * to end of rnd; join with sl st—18 sc.

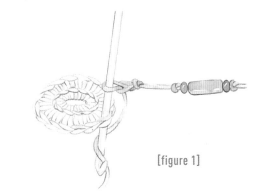

[figure 1]

RND 3: Ch 1, *sc 2 in first st, sc 2; repeat from * to end of rnd; join with sl st—24 sc. Fasten off and weave in ends.

assembly

Be sure to lay out the crocheted circles on the strands before assembling the necklace. This will allow you to arrange them in an aesthetically pleasing manner.

1. Cut 2½ yd (2.3 m) of caribou-colored yarn, coat end lightly with glue, roll into a point, and let dry (this will make it easier to string beads).

2. At the other end of the yarn leave a tail of at least 6" (15 cm) and add bead group as follows: *Tie an overhand knot; string 1 seed bead, 1 wood cylinder bead, and 1 seed bead. Tie an overhand knot so that the beads are snug between knots (see Tip on p. 73).

3. Repeat from * to add desired amount of beads (1–3 groups total).

4. Crochet one of the one-, two-, or three-round circles onto the yarn below the beads as follows:

   Make slipknot, ch 1, *insert hook through a stitch of last round of circle from top to bottom, ch through [figure 1].

   Repeat from * to ch through circle, inserting hook through sts across center of circle.

   Ch 1 on opposite side of circle; pass yarn through end loop to fasten off.

5. Repeat Step 2 to add desired number of bead groups, leaving space between groups to your taste (I differed the arrangement of space and bead groups at random between crocheted circles to create visual interest).

6. Repeat Step 4 to add another crocheted circle of any size (or try adding 2 of different sizes stacked together).

7. Continue repeating Steps 2 and 4, arranging to your taste, until you have just under one-third of the beads (about 21 wood cylinder beads and 42 seed beads) and 7 crocheted circles on the strand. Tie an overhand knot snug against the last bead on the strand and set aside.

8. Repeat Steps 1–7 to create a second strand (while arranging bead groups and crocheted circles, keep in mind the desired finished length of the strands. You may want them to be different lengths, in which case you may want to place elements closer on one strand, and farther apart on another. Also keep in mind that the 3-to-1 connectors will cause the top strand to hang higher than those below). Repeat Steps 1–7 to create a third strand using about 23 wood cylinder beads, 46 seed beads, and 11 crocheted circles.

9. Use one end of one of the shorter strands to string 1 knot cup and 1 seed bead. Tie an overhand knot around the seed bead, trim the yarn, and fold the knot cup around the knot and bead. Repeat the entire step for the other end of the strand.

10. Attach the knot cup to one loop of one 3-to-1 connector, using round-nose pliers to curl the knot cup loop around the connector's loop. Repeat the entire step for the other end of the strand, making sure you attach the knot cup to the loop of the other 3-to-1 connector that is the mirror image of the first connector.

11. Repeat Steps 9 and 10 using another strand and the middle loops of the connectors. Repeat Steps 9 and 10 using the last strand and the remaining loops of the connectors.

12. Open one jump ring and string the top loop of one 3-to-1 connector and the ring half of the clasp.

13. Open one jump ring and string a second jump ring and the toggle half of the clasp. Open the last jump ring and string the jump ring just used and top loop of the remaining 3-to-1 connector.

---

tip

* If you find it difficult to get the knots snug up against the beads, use the following technique:

1. Create a loose overhand knot near the bead, then use an awl to move the loop up against the bead [figure A].

2. Begin to tighten the knot with the awl still in the loop, using it as necessary to snug the knot against the bead. Remove the awl once you can no longer tighten the knot further with it in place, then finish tightening the knot [figure B].

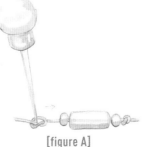

[figure A]

[figure B]

falling leaves scarf necklace

I love green, the color of beautiful leaves and lush forests. So really, how could I resist combining my favorite color with some of my other favorite elements to make a necklace? The amazing stainless steel-and-merino–blend yarn produced a lovely not-quite-solid effect when knitted. Shimmering Czech glass beads brought the leaf shapes to life. The resulting necklace is incredibly light and airy; a pretty reminder of my favorite grove of trees.

materials

YARN
Laceweight (#0 Lace) stainless steel blend
Shown: Habu Textiles, A-148 1/17.6 wool/stainless steel (75% wool, 25% stainless steel; 547 yd [492 m]/ 1 oz [28 g]): #56 green, about 150 yd (137.2 m [3.6 oz]).

* About 5¾ yd (5.3 m) gold 32–34-gauge craft wire

* About 190 topaz AB (aurora borealis) size 9° Czech glass 3-cut seed beads

* About 190 gold matte metallic size 8° hex cut seed beads

needles
* Size 0 (2mm) metal dpns.

notions
* Waste yarn for provisional cast-on; sharp tapestry or sewing needle; flush or side cutters.

gauge
* 40 sts and 38 rows = 4" (10 cm) in st st. Exact gauge is not critical.

finished size
* 2½" (6.5 cm) at widest point x 58" (147.5 cm) long.

need to know

leaf end *(make 2)*

1. With waste yarn, CO 5 sts using provisional CO. Change to working yarn.

2. (WS) Purl 1 row.

3. Work Rows 1–42 of Chart A, a total of 5 times, end on WS Row 6 of Chart A—216 rows.

4. Change to Chart B; work Rows 1–30 once—45 sts. Work Rows 1–30 once.

5. BO as follows: (RS) *k2, slip 2 sts back to left-hand needle, ssk using the same 2 sts; repeat from * until all stitches are BO.

6. Finger block end so that it flares and curls.

chart a

ROWS 1, 3, AND 5: knit.

ROW 2 AND ALL WS ROWS: purl.

ROW 7 (RS): k2, yo, k1-tbl, yo, k2—7 sts

ROW 9 (RS): k3, yo, k1-tbl, yo, k3—9 sts

ROW 11 (RS): k4, yo, k1-tbl, yo, k4—11 sts

ROW 13 (RS): k5, yo, k1-tbl, yo, k5—13 sts

ROW 15 (RS): k6, yo, k1-tbl, yo, k6—15 sts

ROW 17 (RS): k7, yo, k1-tbl, yo, k7—17 sts

ROW 19 (RS): k8, yo, k1-tbl, yo, k8—19 sts

ROWS 21, 23, 25, AND 27 (RS): knit

ROW 29 (RS): k8, sk2p, k8—17 sts

ROW 31 (RS): k7, sk2p, k7—15 sts

ROW 33 (RS): k6, sk2p, k6—13 sts

ROW 35 (RS): k5, sk2p, k5—11 sts

ROW 37 (RS): k4, sk2p, k4—9 sts

ROW 39 (RS): k3, sk2p, k3—7 sts

ROW 41 (RS): k2, sk2p, k2—5 sts

ROW 42 (WS): purl

Repeat rows 1–42 a total of 5 times, and then work rows 1-6, end WS row.

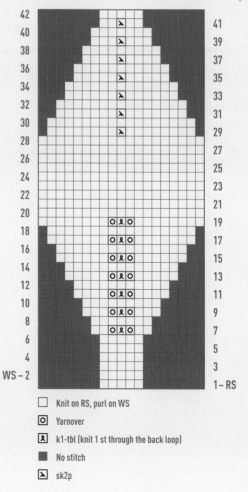

chart a
(5 sts, increased to 19 sts, decreased to 5 sts; 42-row rep)

☐ Knit on RS, purl on WS

⊡ Yarnover

⊠ k1-tbl (knit 1 st through the back loop)

■ No stitch

⊠ sk2p

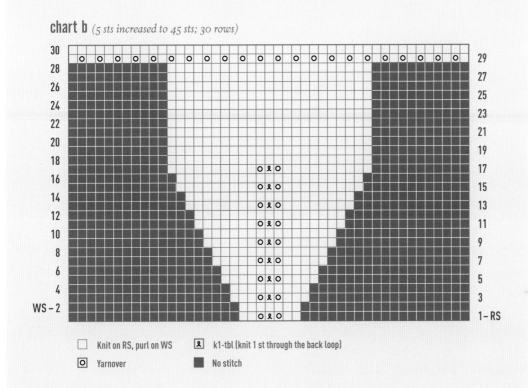

chart b *(5 sts increased to 45 sts; 30 rows)*

Legend:
- ☐ Knit on RS, purl on WS
- ☑ k1-tbl (knit 1 st through the back loop)
- ⊙ Yarnover
- ■ No stitch

chart b

ROW 1 (RS): k2, YO, k1-tbl, YO, k2—7 sts

ROW 2 AND ALL WS ROWS: purl

ROW 3 (RS): k3, YO, k1-tbl, YO, k3—9 sts

ROW 5 (RS): k4, YO, k1-tbl, YO, k4—11 sts

ROW 7 (RS): k5, YO, k1-tbl, YO, k5—13 sts

ROW 9 (RS): k6, YO, k1-tbl, YO, k6—15 sts

ROW 11 (RS): k7, YO, k1-tbl, YO, k7—17 sts

ROW 13 (RS): k8, YO, k1-tbl, YO, k8—19 sts

ROW 15 (RS): K9, YO, k1-tbl, YO, k9—21 sts

ROW 17 (RS): K10, YO, k1-tbl, YO, k10—23 sts

ROWS 19, 21, 23, 25, AND 27 (RS): knit

ROW 29 (RS): k1, *YO, k1; repeat from * to end—45 sts

ROW 30 (WS): purl

Work Rows 1–30 a total of 1 time.

center

Steps 7–9 are worked twice, each using the provisional CO sts of a Leaf End.

7. Pick up stitches from provisional CO—5 sts.

8. Work Rows 7–19 of Chart A—19 sts.

9. Change to st st; work 200 rows (or 21" [53.5 cm]), end WS row.

   Cut yarn, leaving an 18" (46 cm) tail, and sts live on a dpn.

10. Graft live sts from each Leaf End together using Kitchener stitch. Weave in ends with a sharp tapestry or sewing needle, being sure to pass yarn through itself to hold in place.

bead wraps

11. Use 15½" (39.5 cm) segments of wire to string beaded wraps in narrow sections between leaves in the following manner: Weave one end of the wire through knitted material so that about 5½" (13.5 cm) of wire is sticking out at the other end, and about ¾" (2 cm) of wire is woven into the knitted material [figure 1].

12. Mix topaz aurora borealis and gold matte metallic beads together and string 30–32 beads onto the long tail wire in a random color arrangement.

13. Wrap the beaded wire around the first narrow knitted section, over the wire woven through the knitted material so that it is covered [figure 2].

[figure 1]

[figure 2]

* As experienced lace knitters know, it is impossible to create symmetrical increases and decreases that look exactly the same. To that end, this scarf necklace is worked in two identical pieces and grafted together using Kitchener stitch in the center. Each piece begins with a provisional cast-on, which is then picked up and knit in the reverse direction. This type of construction allows all increases to be worked as yarnovers.

* Finger block constantly as you are working (while the piece is still on the needles).

14. Twist the wire tails together and run them back under the beads and through the knitting once again to secure. Trim the wire, and tuck the tails underneath the beads.

15. Repeat Steps 11–14 for each remaining narrow knitted section (you will have 12 bead wraps total).

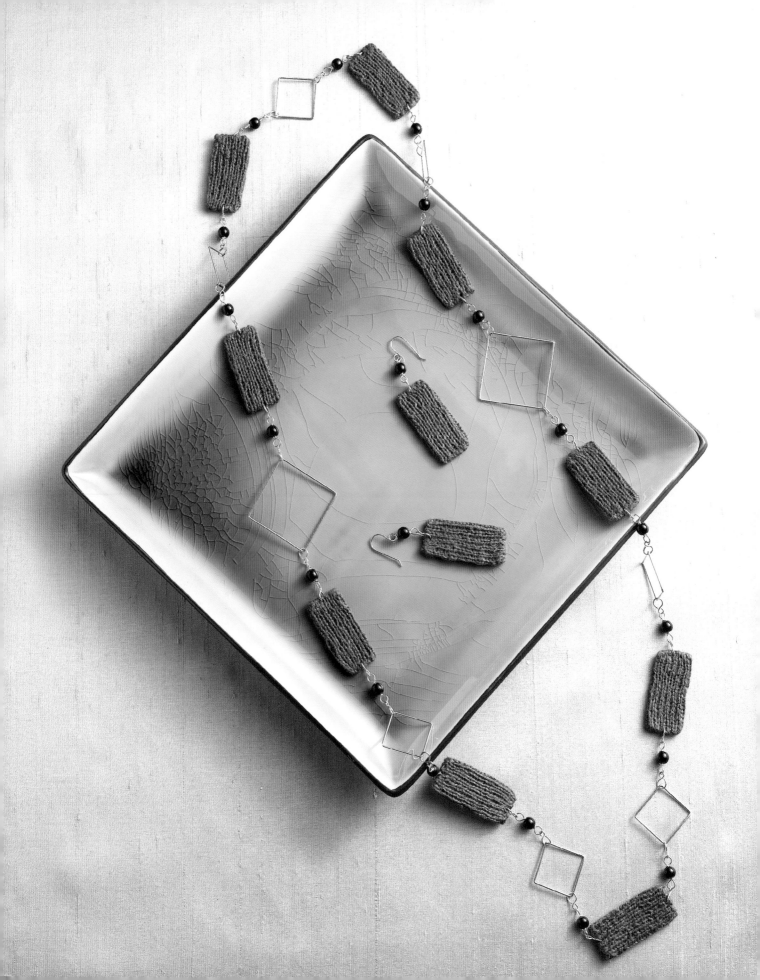

geometry necklace & earrings

I love clean lines and shapes.
Admittedly, I've always been a bit of a geometry geek, so when this design popped into my head, I knew it was my love of geometric shapes speaking! These fun pieces are enhanced by the great sheen and texture of the linen yarn. And what I particularly love is that you can't really tell that this is a knitted piece until you look closely. It's your own little secret.

materials

YARN
Laceweight (#0 Lace [*14/2]) cotton, linen, or hemp
Shown: Louet North America, 14/2 Linen (100% linen; 1,300 yd [1,183 m] per ½ lb [225 g]): #46 cedarwood, 40 yd (36.5 m) for necklace, 10 yd (9.2 m) for earrings.

NECKLACE
* 45" (114.5 cm) of silver-plated 18-gauge copper craft wire

* 36 sterling silver figure-eight connectors

* 45" (114.5 cm) of sterling silver 22-gauge wire

* 18 black 6mm Czech glass round beads

* 7 sterling silver 18-gauge 21mm square wire links

* 2 sterling silver 18-gauge 35mm square wire links

EARRINGS
* 10" (25.5 cm) silver-plated 18-gauge copper craft wire

* 2 sterling silver figure-eight connectors

* 6" (15 cm) sterling silver 22-gauge wire

* 2 black 6mm Czech glass round beads

* 1 pair sterling silver ear wires

needles
* Size 0 (2.25 mm) metal dpns.

tools
* Round-nose pliers; flat-nose and/or chain-nose pliers; flush or side cutters; nylon jaw pliers; tapestry needle; scissors; ball peen hammer and bench block; standard Tic Tac container (measures about 1½ x 2 ½" [3.8 x 6.5 cm]).

gauge
* 9 sts and 15 rows = 1" (3 cm) unstretched in st st.

finished size

* Necklace: 44½" (113 cm).

* Earrings (including ear wires): ¾" (2 cm) wide x 2¾" (7 cm) long.

necklace

wire rectangles *(make 9)*

1. Without pre-cutting the wire, wrap about 5"
(12.5 cm) of 18-gauge craft wire around Tic Tac
container [figure 1] and cut with flush cutters, leaving 1" (2.5 cm) of wire overlapping. Slide the wire
off the end of the container.

2. Using chain-nose or flat-nose pliers, bend the ends
of wire at the corner 45° into the middle of the rectangle [figure 2].

3. Wrap one wire tail firmly around the other twice,
and trim [figure 3].

4. Using flat-nose pliers, square up the corners by
grasping the wire at the corner and pressing the
adjacent wire against the pliers [figure 4].

5. Hammer the rectangle with the flat side of the ball
peen hammer on the bench block to harden the
wire.

[figure 1]

[figure 2]

[figure 3]

[figure 4]

notes

* Knitted fabric is stretched tight over wire. Gauge must be
  sufficiently tight to produce negative ease around the wire
  framework.

* Less expensive silver-plated copper wire is used for the covered
  rectangles, rather than sterling silver wire, because the wire will
  not show.

* These little rectangles are knit in the round, but regular seams
  are just too bulky for these delicate pieces. To achieve a
  seamless look, the rectangles are worked just like you would
  work the toe of a sock, by finishing the two open ends with the
  Kitchener stitch and the invisible horizontal seam.

knitted envelopes *(make 9)*

6. With yarn and dpns, leaving an 8" (20.5 cm) tail, CO 12 sts as follows: begin with a lark's head knot and CO 10 sts using the backward-loop CO method.

7. Turn and knit one row, evenly distributing stitches across 4 dpns to begin knitting with 5 dpns.

8. Join for working in the round, being careful not to twist stitches. Work 20 rnds in st st.

9. Divide stitches evenly onto 2 dpns; cut yarn, leaving an 8" (20.5 cm) tail.

10. Using a tapestry needle, graft the live stitches from each dpn together using the Kitchener stitch.

11. Tie yarn off and thread yarn back inside rectangle. Pull tail end through knitted fabric and trim.

12. Insert a wire rectangle into the CO end of the knitted envelope.

13. Stretch the knitting to accommodate the rectangle. Using a tapestry needle, sew the bottom seams with the invisible horizontal seam.

14. Tie yarn off and thread yarn back inside rectangle. Pull tail end through knitted fabric and trim.

tip

* 14/2 (see materials on p. 81) is the classification used by weavers for the weight of yarn featured in this project. It is equivalent to the CYCA Laceweight (#0 Lace) classification used by knitters and crocheters.

assemble components *(make 9)*

15. Using a tapestry needle, make a hole in the center of one short end of a knitted rectangle inside the wire frame. Open the large end of a figure-eight connector as you would a jump ring and attach it to the rectangle through the hole just made [figure 5].

16. Repeat Step 15 on the other end of the knitted rectangle.

[figure 5]

beaded links

Create wrapped-loop links with beads in the following manner:

17. Use 2½" (6.25 cm) of sterling silver 22-gauge wire and round-nose pliers to form a wrapped loop that attaches to the small end of one of the figure-eight connectors of a knitted rectangle. Trim the wire.

18. String 1 round bead and form a wrapped loop. Trim the wire.

19. Repeat Steps 17 and 18 until 9 rectangles have one wrapped-loop link on each side (you will have 18 wrapped-loop links with beads and 18 remaining figure-eight connectors).

20. Open the small end of a figure-eight connector as you would a jump ring and string the free loop of one of the Beaded Links just made [figure 6]. Repeat until all 9 rectangles have a figure-eight connector attached to the Beaded Links on both sides.

[figure 6]

assemble necklace

21. Open the large end of one of the figure-eight connectors (attached to Beaded Link in previous steps) and string one 21mm square link.

22. Repeat Step 21 on the opposite side of the knitted rectangle just used, attaching a second 21mm square link to the figure-eight connector.

23. Repeat Steps 21 and 22 until you have a strand of four knitted rectangles attached to each other with three 21mm square links (see image on p. 80). Set aside.

24. Repeat Steps 21 and 22 to create a second strand of 5 knitted rectangles attached to each other with four 21mm square links.

25. To complete the necklace, connect the two strands by attaching the large loops of the free figure-eight connectors at the end of the strands to the 35mm square links (see image on p. 80).

earrings

wire rectangles *(make 2)*

1. Repeat Steps 1–5 on p. 82 to make Wire Rectangles.

knitted envelopes *(make 2)*

2. Repeat Steps 6–14 on p. 83 to make Knitted Envelopes.

assemble earrings *(make 2)*

3. With 1 Wire Rectangle, repeat Step 15, then repeat Steps 17 and 18 on p. 84.

4. Open the small loop of the figure-eight connector attached to the knitted rectangle, as you would a jump ring and string one loop of the Beaded Link.

5. Open the bottom loop of 1 ear wire as you would a jump ring and string the free loop of the beaded link just used.

felt

I have to admit that I have always thought of felt as, well, chunky. At least I did until I began experimenting with lighter yarns and adding beads. Suddenly, so many possibilities became apparent! This section was undoubtedly challenging to design, but, at the same time, incredibly satisfying because it blew my previous conceptions about felt right out the window. I've used knitting, crochet, needlefelting, and wet felting to present some pieces that I think will stretch your image of felt as well!

This felted necklace posed a challenge for me at first. It needed to be a delicate piece, but not all yarns lend themselves to creating delicate felt. I tried all sorts of different weights of yarn. Nothing looked quite right. And then I tried felting a laceweight yarn. I was hooked! The crocheted rounds are small, and the laceweight yarn was so quick to felt that they hardly took any time at all. The result was a beautiful and delicate felted necklace, with just a little sparkle added by the elegant teardrop beads.

materials

YARN

Laceweight (#0 Lace) wool and laceweight (#0 Lace [*14/2]) linen

Shown: Trendsetter Yarns, Cashwool from Lane Borgosesia (100% merino wool, 1,460 yd [1,335 m]/3.5 oz [100 g]): #11 black, 1 hank; #26904 celery green, 1 hank.

Shown: Louet North America, Euroflax 14/2 Linen (100% linen, 530 yd [484.6]/3.5 oz [100 g]): #22 black, about 10 yd (9.1 mm).

NECKLACE

* 150 granite mixture 3.4mm Miyuki teardrop beads
* 2 silver-plated (lead-free pewter) 4x6mm oval jump rings
* 1 silver-plated 18mm square art deco toggle clasp
* 2 silver-plated 7mm jump rings
* 2 silver-plated (lead-free pewter) 8mm faceted cone bead caps
* 7" (18 cm) of silver-plated 18-gauge wire

hook

* Size 3 (2.1 mm) steel.

tools

* Big Eye beading needle; G-S Hypo Cement; round-nose pliers; chain-nose pliers; flush or side cutters; sewing needle.

gauge

* Exact gauge is not critical.

finished size

* 18¼" (46.5 cm).

need to know

Abbreviations **p. 118**
Overhand Knot **p. 118**
Crochet Basics **pp. 121–122**
Double Crochet (dc) **p. 122**
Wet-Felting Laceweight Yarn **p. 93**
Stringing **p. 123**
Wrapped Loop **p. 124**

necklace

black rounds *(make 5)*

1. Using 2 strands of black wool yarn held together and size 3 steel hook, ch 15, sl st into first ch (ring made).

   RND 1: Ch 2 (not included in final st count), dc 30 in ring; sl st into tch to join—30 dc.

   RND 2: Ch 1 (not included in final st count), *sc 2, 2 sc in next dc; rep from * to end of rnd; sl st into tch to join—40 sc.
   Fasten off. Measurement before felting: about 1⅛" (2.8 cm) in diameter.

2. Handfelt rounds (see instructions on p. 93). Measurement after felting: about 1" (2.5 cm) in diameter.

green rounded squares *(make 7)*

3. Using 2 strands of green wool yarn held together and size 3 steel hook, ch 16, sl st into first ch (ring made).

   RND 1: Ch 2 (not included in final st count), dc 32 in ring; sl st to tch to join—32 dc.

   RND 2: Ch 1 (not included in final st count), [sc 3, 2 sc in next dc, sc, 2 sc in next dc, sc 2] 4 times, sl st to tch to join—40 sc.
   Fasten off. Measurement before felting: about 1½" (3.2 cm) in diameter.

4. Felt rounded squares (see instructions on p. 93). Measurement after felting: about 1" (2.5 cm) square.

beaded chains *(make 3)*

5. Using the Big Eye beading needle and black linen yarn, string 150 teardrop beads in random color order.

6. Ch for 33½" (85 cm), placing beads randomly by moving bead up against crochet hook and catching in next ch.

7. Wet and stretch to straighten kinks, if necessary. Make sure that the final strand measures 33½" (85 cm) when stretched straight.

assembly

8. Use one 4×6mm oval jump ring to connect the bar half of the clasp to the other 4×6mm oval jump ring. Attach one 7mm jump ring to the 4×6mm jump ring. Attach the other 7mm jump ring to the ring half of the clasp. Set aside for use in Step 14.

9. Thread the long beaded chain in and out of the felted rounds (black) and squares (green) by passing the chain through the holes as seen in [figure 1], in the following order:
1st chain: round, square, round, square.
2nd chain: square, round, square, square.
3rd chain: round, square, square, round.

You will be able to slide the felted pieces up and down the necklace for desired positioning. Place felted pieces in the center of each strand so there is about 5½" (14 cm) of beaded chain on each end.

10. Tie the ends of one of the chains together with an overhand knot and saturate the knot with G-S Hypo Cement. Let dry and trim ends. Repeat for remaining 2 chains. You now have 3 completed strands.

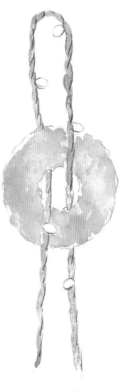

[figure 1]

∗ 14/2 (see Materials on p. 89) is the classification used by weavers for the weight of yarn featured in this project. It is equivalent in weight, but not necessarily in strength, to the CYCA Laceweight (#0 Lace) classification used by knitters and crocheters.

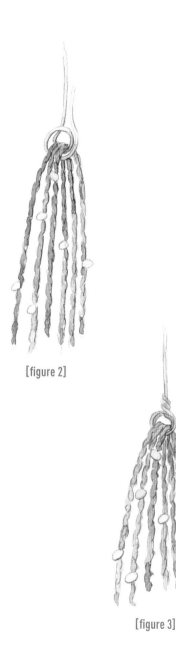

[figure 2]

[figure 3]

11. Use the widest part of round-nose pliers to grip the center of 3½" (9 cm) of 18-gauge wire. Wrap the wire around the pliers to form an elongated U shape. Hold the center of each of the 3 strands of beaded chain and slide them into the U. Gently place the round-nose pliers on top of the beaded chains and wrap each end of the wire 180° around the pliers [figure 2].

12. Bend one of the wires so that it is at a 90° bend from the other wire. Wrap the bent wire around the straight wire twice to form two coils. Trim the tail end of the coiled wire with flush cutters [figure 3]. Use the remaining wire to string 1 bead cap, making sure that all knots are hidden underneath the bead caps [figure 4]. Form a wrapped loop.

13. Open one 7mm jump ring and string the wrapped loop just made and one side of the toggle clasp.

14. Repeat Steps 11–13 for the other side of the necklace.

[figure 4]

wet-felting laceweight yarn

The laceweight yarn used in this piece felts so quickly that, even though it is not beaded, it is not advisable to put it in the washing machine. I handfelted all of the donut pieces in about half an hour. Simply rub the pieces between your hands in a circular motion with hot soapy water (a drop or two of mild detergent should do the trick, if you get too much, the fibers won't bond well). After the pieces have felted, shock them by rinsing or submerging in cold water. Then back to the sink full of hot water. You can abuse them mercilessly, but be sure to stretch them to the desired shape for drying. If they dry while crushed, they may not be salvageable.

When I saw the leather ends on this cuff, it was love at first sight. I could not rest until I had found a way to use them! So I experimented with different jewelry styles, playing with bead and wire combinations. But the leather ends seemed to overpower anything I added to the cuff. And then it hit me: felt! Once I made a test strand, I knew it was meant to be. The cuff was so quick and fun to make that I absolutely could not resist making a necklace as well!

materials

YARN
Worsted-weight (#4 medium) wool
Shown: Cascade Yarns, Wool 220 (100% wool; 220 yd [201.2 m]/3.5 oz [100 g]): #8555 black, 1 hank.

CUFF
* 110 metallic purple, bronze, and brass-colored size 6° seed beads
* 10 brass 6x5mm coil ends
* black 50x60mm 5-hole leather end with snap closure

NECKLACE
* 370 metallic purple, bronze, and brass-colored size 6° seed beads
* 7" (18 cm) of gold-plated 18-gauge wire
* 2 gold-plated 8x8mm end caps
* 3 gold-plated 6mm jump rings
* 1 gold-plated (lead-free pewter) toggle clasp

hook
* Size H/8 (5 mm).

notions and tools
* Big Eye beading needle; round-nose pliers; flat-nose pliers; chain-nose pliers; flush or side cutters; tapestry needle; small crochet hook (to pull yarn through coil ends); 3 knitting needles (for twisting necklace strands).

gauge
* Chain of 22 stitches = 5½" (14 cm), before felting; about 4¾" (12 cm), after felting. Exact gauge is not critical.

finished size
* Necklace, including clasp: 16.5" (42 cm). Felted portion only: 14.5" (37 cm).
* Bracelet: 2" (4 cm) wide x 7¾" (19 cm) long.

need to know

multistrand cuff
beaded strands

1. Using Big Eye beading needle and yarn, string 22 size 6° seed beads in random color order.

2. Leaving a tail of at least 6" (15 cm), ch 22, pushing a bead up after each stitch, including the initial slip-knot, and ending with a bead before fastening off.

3. Fasten off, leaving a tail of at least 6" (15 cm).

4. Repeat Steps 1–3 four more times for a total of 5 beaded strands.

5. Handfelt strands (see instructions on p. 99) until chain stitches are invisible. Twist and pull wet-felted strands until they are straight. Let strands dry completely.

assembly

6. Insert a small crochet hook through 1 brass coil end (from the loop side) and pull end of beaded strand all the way through coil [figure 1].

7. Repeat Step 6 for one end of all beaded strands and leave all strands loose inside coils.

8. Use flat-nose and chain-nose pliers to open the loop of each coil end as you would a jump ring and string the holes of one leather end, making sure that the smooth side of the leather end and the beads of the strands are all facing up.

9. Repeat Steps 6–9 for the free ends of all strands and using remaining leather end. Make sure that both leather ends and all beads are facing up (do not twist strands). Adjust so that all strands are equal in length before completing Step 10.

10. Using chain-nose pliers, squeeze the bottom ends of the coils (opposite of the loops) so that they sink into the beaded strands.

11. Trim ends of strands flush with end of coil under the loop.

[figure 1]

necklace
beaded strand

1. With Big Eye beading needle and yarn, string 370 size 6° seed beads in random color order.

2. Leaving a tail of at least 6" (15 cm), ch, pushing a bead up after each stitch, including the initial slipknot, and ending with a bead before fastening off, until all beads are used.

3. Fasten off. Cut yarn, then join to the other end of the chain with a square knot, making sure not to let the strand twist. Weave in ends.

4. Handfelt strand (see instructions on p. 99). Once felted, hang strand to dry. Strand should measure about 82" (2 m).

tips

* It is a good idea to buy a few more of the brass 6x5mm coil ends than you need for the bracelet, since the loops are sometimes brittle and can easily break.

* Be aware that not all beads are created equally. When choosing beads for this project, make sure your beads are colorfast and that the material can withstand being submerged in water. If you are not sure of the appropriateness of the beads, make a small felted sample including a few of the beads. This will save you money and frustration!

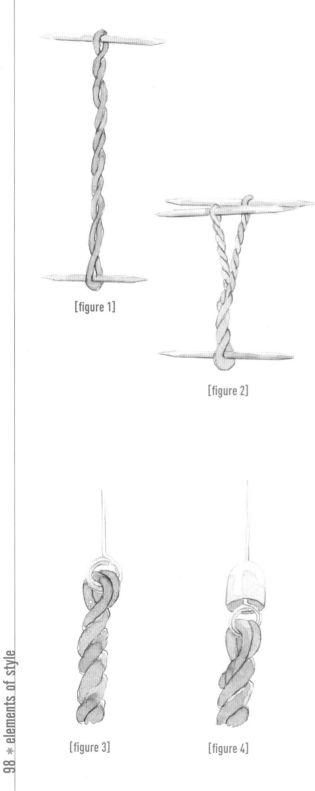

[figure 1]

[figure 2]

twisting strand

5. Stretch strand between two knitting needles and twist one needle (figure 1) until strand begins to twist back on itself.

6. Insert third knitting needle at the midpoint of the twisted strand to hold it and let the strand twist back on itself (figure 2).

7. Use the widest part of round-nose pliers to grip 3½" (9 cm) of 18-gauge wire ½" (1.3 cm) from one end. Wrap the wire around the pliers to form an enlongated J shape. Slip both end loops of the twisted strand off of the knitting needle and onto the wire. Use round-nose pliers to grasp the short end of the wire and form a simple loop around the strand and the pliers, then loop around again to form a double simple loop and trim the short wire (figure 3).

8. Use flat-nose pliers to grasp the longer end of the wire near the loop and bend it straight up. String 1 end cap onto the wire (figure 4) and snug it down tightly over the strands. Form a wrapped loop and trim the wire.

9. Repeat Steps 18–19 on the other end of the necklace.

10. Use 1 jump ring to attach 1 wrapped loop to the ring half of the clasp. Attach 1 jump ring to the other wrapped loop. Use 1 jump ring to attach the jump ring just used to the bar half of the clasp.

[figure 3]

[figure 4]

handfelting beaded strands

Felting a beaded piece requires extra care. Do not felt beaded pieces in the washing machine as the beads may break. In order to successfully felt beaded strands, rub the strands between your palms, as if you were forming a rope made of clay. Fill a sink halfway with hot (not burning hot) water and add a little dishwashing soap or wool wash. Submerge the strand and begin rubbing it between your palms. Keep working your way down the strand of beads, going around and around. At intervals, shock the whole strand in cold water and then return it to the hot water for more rubbing. Keep up the felting motion until you have the desired effect, then remove from the water, pat with a towel to remove excess water, and hang to dry. I weighted the strands by hanging a coat hanger from the ends of the strands. This ensured an even length and appearance after drying.

This little bracelet began as an experiment, but by the time it was finished, it had taken on a life of its own. It is a wonderfully portable project, with rings crocheted in laceweight yarn. The materials are so light and small that I packed them and took my little project along with me to all sorts of activities with my kids. Once the pieces have been felted, there is a fun, quick, and simple foray into needlefelting. I'm not sure which was more enjoyable—making this bracelet or wearing it!

materials

YARN
Laceweight (#0 Lace) wool
Shown: Trendsetter Yarns, Cashwool from Lane Borgosesia (100% merino wool, 1,460 yd [1,335 m]/3.5 oz [100 g]): #11 black, 1 hank.

FIBER
Wool roving.
Shown: Ashford New Zealand Carded Sliver (100% wool): periwinkle, lilac haze, and smoke (most retailers sell roving by the ounce).

* 2 black 7x13mm faceted rondelles

* 16 black size 11° seed beads

* 2 silver-plated 2" (50 mm) head pins

* 6" (15 cm) of Soft Flex .014 fine beading wire (nylon-coated stainless steel)

* 2 silver-plated 2mm crimp beads

* 2 silver-plated wire guardians

hook

* Size 3 (2.1 mm) steel hook.

tools and notions

* Felting needle; round-nose pliers; chain-nose pliers; flush or side cutters; sewing needle; G-S Hypo Cement.

gauge

* Exact gauge is not critical.

finished size

* 2" (5 cm) wide x 7.5" (19 cm) long.

need to know

cuff

black circles *(make 12)*

1. Using 2 strands of yarn held together, ch 15, sl st into first ch (ring made).

RND 1: Ch 2 (not included in final st count), dc 30 in ring; sl st into tch to join—30 dc.

RND 2: Ch 1 (not included in final st count), *sc 2, 2 sc in next dc; rep from * to end of rnd; sl st into tch to join—40 sc.

Fasten off. Measurement before felting: about 1⅛" (2.8 cm) in diameter.

2. Handfelt circle (see instructions on p. 93). Measurement after felting: about 1" (2.5 cm) in diameter.

needlefelt embellishment

3. Use the felting needle to needlefelt roving onto 3 black circles (see instructions on p. 103), one each in smoke, periwinkle, and lilac haze.

clasp

wrapped-loop buttons *(make 2)*

4. Use 1 head pin to string 1 seed bead and 1 rondelle. Form a wrapped loop.

assembly

5. Use the beading wire to string 1 crimp bead, 1 seed bead, and the first hole of 1 wire guardian. Use the wire guardian to string 1 Wrapped-Loop Button **[figure 1]**, then use the wire to string the other hole of the wire guardian and 1 seed bead. Pass back through the crimp bead. Pull the beading wire snug and flatten the crimp bead with chain-nose pliers. Trim the short tail wire with flush cutters.

6. String 10 seed beads onto the beading wire.

7. Repeat Step 5.

[figure 1]

tips

* Don't poke the needle too forcefully into the piece when needlefelting. You don't want your needle sinking too far into the mat underneath; it is just a barrier to protect your needle and the surface you are working on.

* Be sure to watch out for your fingers! The barbed felting needles are very sharp.

* If your felt is sticking to the mat, gently pull up on the piece (or pull up the towel if you are using one), first around the edges, then work your fingers to the middle to loosen any fibers that have bonded to the mat. You may want to check for bonding as you go along and gently release the portion you have already felted.

finishing

8. With black wool yarn and the sewing needle, whipstitch a row of circles together with WS facing in the following order: black, black, lilac haze, black, black.

Repeat to stitch a row together in the following order: black, periwinkle, black, black, black.

9. With WS facing, whipstitch both rows together so that embellished circles are placed diagonally from each other on RS.

10. With WS facing, whipstitch remaining black circle at one end of the rows so that it is placed equally between both rows. Repeat to attach the remaining embellished circle (smoke) to the opposite end.

To wear your fabulous cuff, insert one Wrapped Loop Button through the circle on one end of bracelet. This side will stay put and the other will act as a clasp when inserted through the opposite side.

needlefelting

For a needlefelting project like this one, with a small surface area, you'll need a single felting needle and a base to felt on. Many craft stores carry needlefelting mats, but you can also use a piece of soft packing foam covered with a thin towel.

First, compact the roving by rubbing it between your palms and then stretch it out. Then lay the fibers over the surface you are felting it onto (in this case, the felted circles) and poke the needle in and out, all over the surface. I used the needle both straight up and down and at an angle.

To ensure that the edges would be smooth, I finished each piece by rolling a small amount of roving into a strand and placed it around the edge, felting it down with the needle as I went along. Trim any excess bits of fluff, and you will have a beautifully finished piece.

ball & chain necklace & earrings

A friend recently sent me a bag of beautiful wool roving. Needless to say, I was immediately engaged in planning all sorts of wonderful ways to use this delicious fiber! Although several ideas came to mind, I knew right away when I had hit on the right one—felt balls. I had to make felt balls. Combining these with some wire tubing I created with my beloved knitting doll was a stroke of genius. The result is a simple but striking necklace that will complement many an outfit. And with matching earrings as well, who can resist this harmonious marriage of wire and fiber?

materials

FIBER

Wool roving
Shown: Louet Dyed Corriedale Top (100% wool): #30 jade, ½ lb; (8 oz); #35 bright blue, ½ lb (8 oz).

* Cotton waste yarn
* 1 spool (30 yd [27.5 m]) of Artistic Wire silver non-tarnish 32-gauge silver-plated copper wire
* 2' (61 cm) of Soft Flex .014 fine beading wire

NECKLACE

* 4' (1.2 m) of 8mm flat round-link silver-plated chain
* 27 silver-plated 4mm round beads
* 18 silver-plated 2mm crimp tubes
* 18 silver-plated wire guardians

EARRINGS

* 4" (10 cm) of silver-plated 8mm flat round-link chain
* 2 silver-plated size 11° seed beads
* 2 silver-plated 4mm round beads
* 4 silver-plated 2mm crimp tubes
* 2 silver-plated wire guardians
* 1 pair silver French ear wires

tools

* Knitting doll or spool knitter with 6-peg capability; flush or side cutters; large embroidery needle; round-nose pliers; chain-nose pliers; crimping pliers; sewing needle.

gauge

* Exact gauge is not critical.

finished size

* Necklace: 45" (114.5 cm).
* Earrings (including ear wires): 3.5" (9 cm).

need to know

Making Felt Balls p. 111

Knitting Doll p. 120

Abbreviations p. 118

Knitting Basics pp. 118–119

Stringing p. 123

Crimping p. 124

necklace

knit cages *(make 6)*

1. Using a knitting doll with 6 pegs, mark beginning of round by placing a small piece of tape near the first peg on the knitting doll.

2. Thread knitting doll with cotton waste yarn and work 2 rnds. Switch to knitting with wire (by simply continuing with wire, right over the waste yarn). Do not tie knots. Work 3 rnds.

3. Cut the wire, leaving a 5" (12.5 cm) tail. Run the wire tail through the live stitches and pull the knitted tube off the knitting doll.

felt balls *(make 6)*

4. Using jade (and just a bit of bright blue) wool roving, make 6 felt balls, each measuring about ⅝" (1.5 cm). See instructions on p. III.

5. Place 1 felt ball into a knit cage. Pull the wire tail to gather stitches. Close one end of the cage by wrapping the wire through stitches and around itself **[figure 1]**. Trim the wire close.

6. Carefully remove the waste yarn from the opposite end of the wire cage. Run the wire tail through the bottom of the live stitches and pull tight.

7. Thread the wire in and out, through several stitches, wrap around the gathered stitches, and trim.

8. Repeat Steps 5–7 to encase the 5 remaining felt balls.

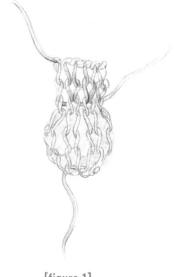

[figure 1]

tips

* Be aware that not all wool roving is alike. If you plan to substitute, you may want to do some experimenting first. That way you can see how the fibers behave before committing yourself to a certain type.

* The whole project actually requires less than 2 ounces of the jade roving and just a tiny bit of the bright blue (but it is sold in 8-ounce increments), so this would be a great way to use up small amounts of roving.

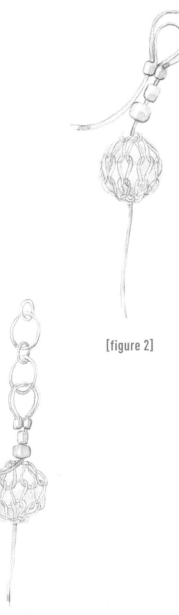

[figure 2]

[figure 3]

assembly

9. Use flush cutters to cut nine 8-link (about 3¾" [9.5 cm]) pieces of flat round-link silver chain.

Felt Ball Sections

10. Thread the .014 beading wire through the embroidery needle. Do not cut wire from spool. Use the needle to string the center of the felt ball, then remove the embroidery needle.

11. String 1 silver-plated 4mm bead, 1 crimp tube, and 1 wire guardian [figure 2].

12. String the end of one piece of 8-link chain onto the wire guardian. Pass beading wire back through the crimp tube and the 4mm bead.

13. Pull the beading wire tight and crimp the crimp tube [figure 3]. Trim the beading wire.

14. Snug the felt ball tight against the 4mm bead from the opposite side and cut beading wire from the spool, leaving a 5" (12.5 cm) tail.

15. Repeat Steps 11–13 for the other side of the same felt ball using the 5" (12.5 cm) wire tail and a second piece of 8-link chain.

16. Use another felt ball to repeat Steps 10–14, attaching the wire guardian to the other end of the second 8-link piece of chain. Repeat Steps 11–13, attaching the wire guardian to a third piece of 8-link chain.

17. You now have a length including three 8-link pieces of chain and 2 caged felt balls; set this aside. Repeat Steps 10–16 twice to form a total of 3 felt ball chains. The felt ball chains will be connected in the following steps.

beaded sections

18. Use 3" (7.5 cm) of .014 beading wire to string 1 crimp tube and 1 wire guardian.

19. Use the wire guardian to string the free end of 1 felt ball chain.

20. Pass beading wire back through the crimp tube and crimp.

21. Using the longer tail of beading wire, string 5 silver-plated 4mm beads, 1 crimp tube, and 1 wire guardian. Pull the beading wire tight through the wire guardian.

22. String the free end of the second felt ball chain onto the wire guardian. Pass back through the crimp tube and crimp. Pass wire tails at both ends through several beads to secure; trim wire.

23. Repeat Steps 18–22 twice more to attach the second felt ball chain to the third felt ball chain and to attach the third felt ball chain to the first felt ball chain, creating a continuous strand.

earrings

wire cages *(make 2)*

1. Using a knitting doll with 6 pegs, mark beginning of round by placing a small piece of tape
near the first peg on the knitting doll.

2. Thread knitting doll with cotton waste yarn and
work 2 rnds. Switch to knitting with wire (by
simply continuing with wire, right over the waste
yarn). Do not tie knots! Work 4 rnds.

3. Run the wire tail the through the live stitches and
pull off the knitting doll. Trim the wire, leaving a
5" (12.5 cm) tail.

felt balls *(make 2)*

4. Make two ⅞" (2.2 cm) felt balls. See instructions
on p. III.

5. Repeat Steps 5–7 on p. 106 to enclose the felt
balls in the knit cages.

assembly

6. Cut the silver flat round-link into two 3-link (1¼" [3.2 cm]) pieces.

7. Use an 8" (20.5 cm) piece of beading wire to thread an embroidery needle. String through the center of 1 felt ball, leaving a 5" (12.5 cm) tail. String 1 size 11° seed bead and pass back through the felt ball [figure 1].

8. Remove the embroidery needle. Use one wire tail to string 1 crimp tube, 1 4mm bead, a second crimp tube, and 1 wire guardian.

9. String the end of one 3-link piece of chain onto the wire guardian.

10. Pass the beading wire back through the crimp tube, 4mm bead, and second crimp tube [figure 2].

11. Use the other wire tail to pass up through the first crimp tube strung, the 4mm bead, and the other crimp tube [figure 3].

12. Snug both lines tight. Crimp both crimp tubes. Trim the beading line.

13. Open the bottom loop of 1 ear wire as you would a jump ring and string the top link of the silver flat round-link chain before closing.

14. Repeat Steps 6–13 for the second earring.

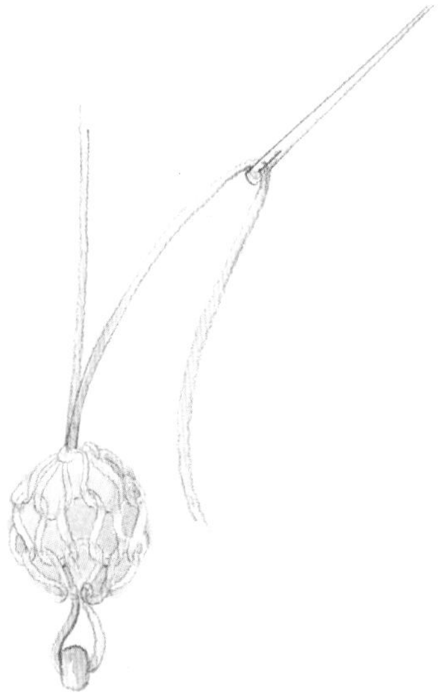

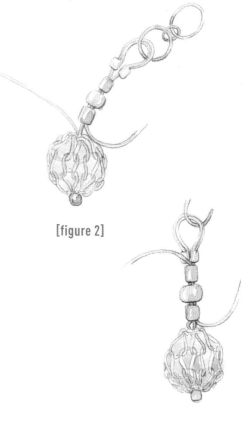

[figure 2]

[figure 1]

[figure 3]

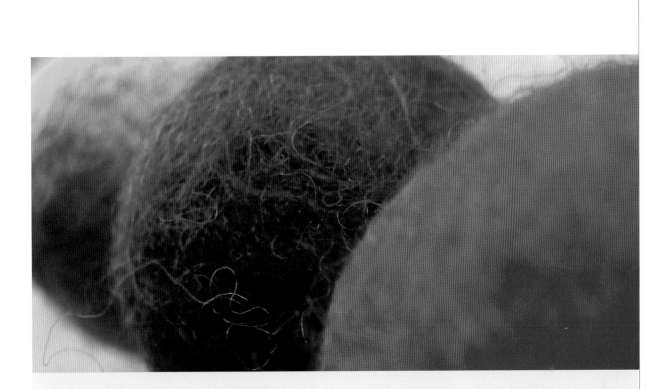

making felt balls

First, get ready with some hot water in a bowl but make sure that the temperature is still comfortable enough for your hands to be submerged in the water; add a few drops of detergent.

Take a small amount of roving and fluff the fiber up until it is puffy and airy, gently rolling it into the general shape of a ball. Next, cup the fiber in both hands and submerge it in the hot soapy water, swishing gently.

After a little while, you will feel the fiber start to shrink a bit. This is good. Keep swishing it around, and when the fiber pulls in further, begin forming the ball by rolling it gently between your palms. Roll in a circular motion to keep the ball even on all sides. (If you have ever hand-rolled truffles,

this is the time to use that experience!) As the ball firms more, begin applying more pressure. You may also dunk the ball in cold water to shock the fiber. Squeeze the cold water out as much as possible, and then put the felt ball back into hot water.

If, after this, you still have surface imperfections, or you'd like the ball to be larger, take a small amount of fiber, spread it out thinly, and wrap it gently around the outside of the ball. Continue to felt the ball as before, being careful to keep it all under water as you felt the fiber to the ball.

Once the ball is felted perfectly, squeeze the water out using a towel. I like drying my felt balls on the heater vent, but if you have a cat, this may not be the best option!

I do not enjoy cutting things up as much as my kids do, but it is still fun, and even liberating, to cut up my knitting! I wasn't sure at first how this concept would work, so I approached it carefully, staring at the felted piece for several days before getting the nerve to begin slicing. In the end, I decided I could make another one fairly quickly if it did not work. But it did work. It was one of those happy occasions when the piece, once realized, was exactly as it had appeared in my mind's eye.

materials

YARN

Worsted weight (#4 Medium)
Shown: Cascade Yarns, Cascade 220 (100% wool; 220 yd [201.2 m]/3.5 oz [100 g]): #8555 black, 1 hank.

* 72 metallic gray/black size 6° seed beads

* 9 silver-plated 4mm round beads

* 1 spool (30 yd [27.5mm]) of Artistic Wire silver non-tarnish 32-gauge silver-plated copper wire

* 2 silver 1" (2.5 cm) D-ring connectors

* 3 silver-plated 9mm jump rings

* 1 silver-plated (lead-free pewter) toggle clasp

needles

* Size 2 (2.75 mm) and size 10½ (6.5 mm) bamboo dpns.

tools and notions

* Round-nose pliers; flat-nose pliers; flush or side cutters; nylon-jaw pliers; utility blade and cutting mat; scissors; sharp tapestry needle; Big Eye beading needle; 2 straight pins; thin but sturdy cardboard.

gauge

* 6 sts and 91 rows in grtr st = about 1¾ x 16½" (4.5 x 42 cm) with larger needles, before felting; 1½ x 15" (3.8 x 38 cm), after felting. Exact gauge is not critical.

finished size

1½" (3.8 cm) wide x 14½" (37.5 cm) long.

need to know

choker

felted portion

A felted swatch is a must for this project! It is important to gauge how thoroughly the knitting needs to be felted in order to cut and sew it without causing the stitches to unravel.

1. Using Big Eye beading needle and yarn, string 72 size 6° seed beads.

2. Using yarn prestrung with beads and larger dpns, CO 6 sts as follows: begin with a lark's head knot and CO 4 sts using thebackward-loop CO method.

3. Work in grtr st as follows for 91 rows (or about 16½" [42 cm]):

ROWS 1–10: K1 tbl, k4, k1 tbl.

ROW 11: Push bead up to needle, k1 tbl working bead into stitch, k4, k1 tbl.

ROWS 12–82: Push bead up to needle, k1 tbl working bead into stitch, p4, k1 tbl.

ROWS 83–91: Rep Row 1.
BO all stitches loosely.

4. Handfelt (follow instructions on p. 117).

5. Smooth and pull felted piece into shape to dry. Felted piece should measure about 1 ½ × 15" (3.8 × 38 cm).

wire inserts *(make 3)*

6. String three 4mm round beads onto wire.

7. With smaller dpns, CO 10 sts as follows: begin with a lark's head knot and CO 8 sts using the backward-loop CO method.

8. Work 10 rows in grtr st, spacing beads out randomly. Finger block piece gently on needle.

9. BO all stitches, weave wire ends in, and trim with flush cutters. Wire pieces should measure about 1 × 1½" (2.5 × 3.8 cm).

tips

* Measure your neck before assembling the choker, determining a length that will fit closely but comfortably around your neck.
* When assembling, be sure to account for the length added by the D-rings and clasp.

placing wire inserts

10. Create a rectangular template from cardboard measuring ⅝ × 1" (1.5 × 2.5 cm).

11. Place choker on a cutting mat and center the rectangle on the felted choker, making sure that there is equal space on both sides and between the top and the bottom edges of the choker.

12. Holding the rectangle firmly in place, cut through the felt with a utility blade, around the sides of the rectangle [figure 1]. If you are not used to using a utility blade, practice first on a swatch or two. If necessary, use scissors to trim the rectangle straight.

13. Measure 1" (2.5 cm) over from both the right and the left edges of the rectangle, and mark each with a straight pin.

14. Place the template with the inside edge against the leftmost pin, again checking that the template is equally spaced between the top and bottom edges of the choker [figure 2]. Use the utility blade to cut through the felt, around the sides of the rectangle.

15. Repeat Step 14, placing the template with the inside edge against the rightmost pin.

[figure 1]

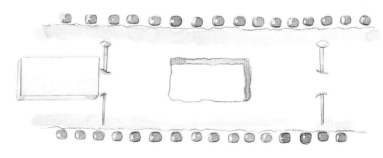

[figure 2]

16. Beginning with the center rectangle, place one wire insert into the cutout and use a tapestry needle and 2 plies of wool yarn to whipstitch the edges of the wire insert to the inside edges of the cutout. Be careful to sew securely and invisibly. Fasten off and weave in end.

17. Repeat Step 16 to attach the other two wire inserts. This side of the choker will become the inside because the choker will look more finished on the opposite side, where the stitching cannot be seen.

assembly

18. Pass one unbeaded end of the felted piece through 1 D-ring, fold it back onto the choker, toward the inside (where the stitching on the wire inserts is more noticeable) of the choker. Using yarn and a tapestry needle, whipstitch the edges down.

19. Repeat Step 18 on the opposite side of the choker, using the remaining D-ring.

20. Use 1 jump ring to connect the ring half of the toggle to 1 D-ring. Attach 1 jump ring to the bar half of the clasp. Use the third jump ring to attach the second jump ring (attached to bar half of the toggle) to the other D-ring.

handfelting garter stitch

The hand motion needed to felt this project is quite unique, and it took me several tries to get it right. Fill a sink halfway with hot soapy water (make sure that the water is still at a comfortable temperature for your hands to be submerged), then fill another sink or a large bowl with cold water.

In order to keep the material flat rather than having it curl, submerge the knitted piece in the hot soapy water, then felt it by folding it over on itself lengthwise and rubbing it up and down between your palms gently. Once felted, shock the fibers by submerging the piece in the cold water, then the hot water, and back into the cold water. Be sure to felt the piece thoroughly so it doesn't ravel when cut.

When you have finished felting, you should not be able to see individual stitches, but you will see a ridge created by the garter stitch. Squeeze any excess water out in a towel and push and pull into shape to dry. Once dry, the dimensions are stable, but while it is still wet, it is easily manipulated.

abbreviations

beg	beginning; begin; begins
BO	bind off
ch	chain
cm	centimeter(s)
CO	cast on
dc	double crochet
dec(s)	decrease(s); decreasing
dpn	double-pointed needles
foll	following; follows
g	gram(s)
grtr st	garter stitch
inc(s)	increase(s); increasing
k	knit
k2tog	knit 2 stitches together (1 stitch decreased)
k3tog	knit 3 stitches together (2 stitches decreased)
mm	millimeter(s)
p	purl
p3tog	purl 3 stitches together (2 stitches decreased)
rem	remain; remaining
rnd(s)	round(s)
RS	right side
sc	single crochet
sl st	slip st
sk2p	skip 1, knit 2 together, pass slip stitch over the knit 2 together (2 stitches decreased)
sp	space(s)
ssk	slip 2 sts, one at a time, as if to knit; replace on left needle and knit together through the back loop (1 stitch decreased)
ssp	slip 2 stitches, one at a time, as if to knit; replace on left needle and purl together through back loop (1 stitch decreased)
st(s)	stitch(es)
st st	stockinette stitch
tbl	through back loops
tch	turning chain
tog	together
WS	wrong side
yd	yard(s)
yo	yarn over
*	repeat starting point
* *	repeat all instructions between asterisks

knots

OVERHAND KNOT

Make a loop with the stringing material. Pass the cord that lies behind the loop over the front cord, then through the loop and pull snug.

SQUARE KNOT

Step 1: Make an overhand knot, passing the right end over the left end.

Step 2: Make another overhand knot, this time passing the left end over the right end. Pull tight.

knitting basics

CAST-ON (CO)

Loop working yarn onto needle to begin knitting. See p. 119 for backward-loop Cast-On method.

KNIT

Step 1: With the working yarn in back of the needle, insert the right needle into the front of the first stitch (the one closest to the tip) from left to right [figure 1].

[figure 1]

Step 2: Now with your right index finger, bring the yarn between the needles from back to front [figure 2].

Step 3: With your right hand, pull the right needle, which now has a loop of yarn around it, toward you and through the stitch, then slip the old stitch off the left needle [figure 3].

Repeat Steps 1–3 until all stitches are knit onto the right needle.

[figure 2]

[figure 3]

PURL

Step 1: Pull the working yarn in front of the needles. Insert the tip of the right needle into the front of the first stitch on the left needle, from right to left [figure 1].

Step 2: Bring the yarn around the front of the right needle and between the needles from right to left and back around the right needle [figure 2].

Step 3: Pull the right needle, with the loop of working yarn around it, and through the stitch on the left needle. Slip the old stitch off the left needle and tighten the new stitch on the right needle [figure 3].

Repeat Steps 1–3 for desired number of stitches.

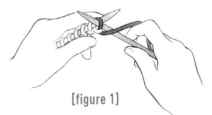

[figure 1]

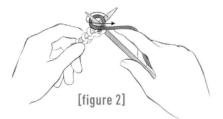

[figure 2]

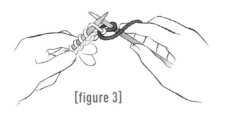

[figure 3]

BIND-OFF (BO)

Knit the first stitch, *knit the next stitch (2 stitches on right needle), insert left needle tip into first stitch on right needle [figure 1] and lift this stitch up and over the second stitch [figure 2] and off the needle [figure 3]. Repeat from * for the desired number of stitches.

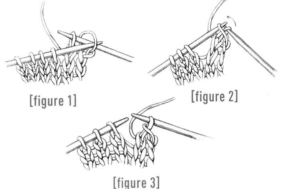

[figure 1]   [figure 2]

[figure 3]

knitting

LARK'S HEAD KNOT

(To begin cast-on) Fold the yarn in half, pass the knitting needle through the fold, then pull the ends of the yarn through the loop created and pull snug.

[figure 1]   [figure 2]

BACKWARD-LOOP CAST-ON

Begin with a lark's head knot, then *make a loop with working yarn and place it on needle backward so that it doesn't unwind. Repeat from * for desired number of stitches.

CABLE CAST-ON

Make a slipknot and place it on left needle. With the right needle, knit into the first stitch on the left needle [figure 1] and place the new stitch onto the left needle [figure 2]. * Insert right needle between first 2 stitches on left needle [figure 3], wrap yarn around needle as if to knit, draw yarn through [figure 4], and place new loop on tip of left needle [figure 5]. Repeat from * for desired number of stitches, always working between the first 2 stitches on the left needle.

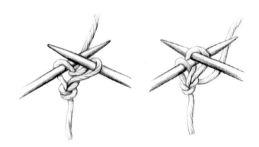

[figure 1]   [figure 2]

[figure 3]   [figure 4]

[figure 5]

PROVISIONAL CAST-ON

Make a loose slipknot of working yarn and place it on the right needle. Hold a length of contrasting waste yarn next to the slipknot and around your left thumb; hold the working yarn over your left index finger. *Bring the right needle forward under the waste yarn, over the working yarn, and grab a loop of working yarn (figure 1), then bring the needle back behind the working yarn and grab a second loop (figure 2). Repeat from * for the desired number of stitches. When you're ready to work in the opposite direction, place the exposed loops on a knitting needle as you pull out the waste yarn.

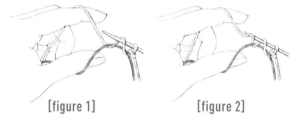

[figure 1]   [figure 2]

GARTER STITCH (GRTR ST)

Garter stitch is the simplest knit pattern and produces a pebblelike surface texture.
Row 1 (RS): Knit.
Row 2: Knit.
Rep Rows 1–2 for pattern.

STOCKINETTE STITCH (ST ST)

Stockinette stitch produces a smooth texture on one side and a pebblelike texture on the other.
Row 1 (RS): Knit.
Row 2: Purl.
Rep Rows 1–2 for pattern.

FINGER BLOCKING

When knitting with wire or wire/fiber blends, stretch the piece out with your fingers after every row or two as you go along. Keeping the piece on the needle, stretch the knitting away from the needle and from side to side until you have evened out the stitches and achieved your desired shape. Blocking in this manner will make it easier to work with the wire or wire/fiber blend once it is knitted.

KNITTING DOLL

Setting up: Bring yarn through center to the top of the knitting doll, holding tail on the bottom with your hand. Wrap yarn around each peg in the counterclockwise direction [figure 1]. *Wrap yarn around each peg once more. Beginning with the first peg, lift the bottom loops over the top loops and off the pegs [figure 2]. Repeat from * to desired length.

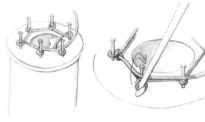

[figure 1]   [figure 2]

JOIN FOR WORKING IN THE ROUND

To begin working in rounds instead of rows, you'll need to join the stitches into a ring. To do this, use the working yarn (attached to the last cast-on stitch) to knit the first cast-on stitch, pulling the two ends of the cast-on row together and forming a circle. Be careful that the cast-on row is not twisted, because it cannot be untwisted once the round is joined. Continue to work each successive stitch in order without turning to work back. There will be a small gap at the join, but this can be effectively tidied up when the cast-on tail is woven in later.

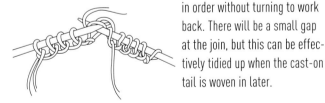

USING FIVE DOUBLE-POINTED NEEDLES

When knitting circularly with five double-pointed needles, the stitches are distributed between four needles and the fifth is used for knitting. Divide the stitches evenly among the four working needles and work the stitches on those needles.

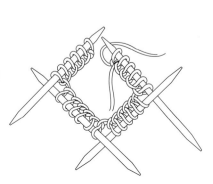

crochet basics

SLIPKNOT

Starting about 4 to 6" (10 to 15 cm) from the end of the yarn, make a loop [figure 1], insert the hook through the loop [figure 2], and gently pull the end to tighten the loop on the hook [figure 3]. Be careful not to pull the end too tightly or you'll be unable to work into this stitch.

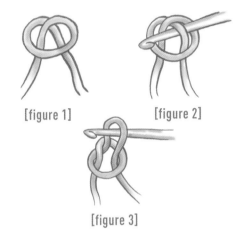

[figure 1]   [figure 2]

[figure 3]

CROCHET CHAIN (CH)

Make a slipknot on the hook. Yarn over hook and draw it through loop of slipknot. Repeat, drawing yarn through the last loop formed.

SINGLE CROCHET (SC)

Insert hook into stitch, yarn over hook and draw a loop through stitch [figure 1], yarn over hook and draw it through both loops on hook [figure 2].

[figure 1]

[figure 2]

DOUBLE CROCHET (DC)

*Yarn over hook, insert hook into a stitch, yarn over hook and draw up a loop (3 loops on hook; figure 1), yarn over hook and draw it through 2 loops [figure 2], yarn over hook and draw it through the remaining 2 loops [figure 3]. Repeat from *.

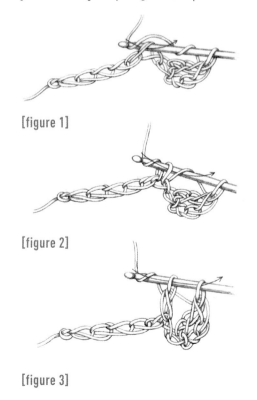

[figure 1]

[figure 2]

[figure 3]

SLIP STITCH CROCHET (SL ST)

*Insert hook into stitch, yarn over hook and draw loop through stitch and loop on hook. Repeat from *.

grafting and stitching

KITCHENER STITCH

Place stitches to be joined on two separate knitting needles. Hold the needles parallel to each other, with the points facing to the right and so that the wrong sides of the knitting face each other. With a threaded tapestry needle, work back and forth between the stitches on the two needles as follows:

Step 1: Bring threaded needle through first stitch on front needle as if to purl and leave stitch on needle.

Step 2: Bring threaded needle through first stitch on back needle as if to knit and leave stitch on needle.

Step 3: Bring threaded needle through first stitch on front needle (the same one used in Step 1) as if to knit and slip this stitch off needle. Bring threaded needle through next stitch on front needle as if to purl and leave stitch on needle.

Step 4: Bring threaded needle through first stitch on back needle as if to purl (as illustrated), slip that stitch off, bring needle through next stitch on back needle as if to knit, and leave this stitch on needle. Repeat Steps 3–4 until all stitches have been worked.

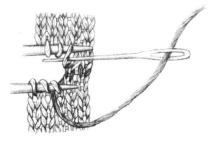

INVISIBLE HORIZONTAL SEAM

Working with the cast-on edges opposite each other, right sides of the knitting facing outward, and working into the stitches just below the bound-off edges, bring threaded tapestry needle out at the center of the first stitch (i.e., go under half of the first stitch) on one side of the seam, then bring needle in and out under the first whole stitch on the other side [figure 1]. *Bring needle into the center of the same stitch it came out of before, then out in the center of the adjacent stitch [figure 2]. Bring needle in and out under the next whole stitch on the other side [figure 3]. Repeat from *, ending with a half-stitch on the first side. Be sure to work along the same row of stitches on each side for a neat line. If the shoulder is sloped and if the final stitches were bound off in steps, there will be a jog or stair-step of two rows between each group of bound-off stitches. To give the seam a smooth appearance in theses cases, do not follow the exact line of stitches just below the bound-off stitches—use the seaming yarn to visually even out the jogs over the distance of two or three stitches.

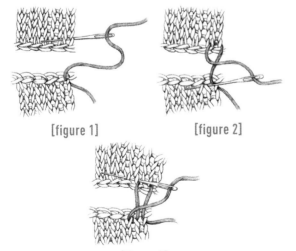

[figure 1]   [figure 2]

[figure 3]

WHIPSTITCH

With right side of work facing and working through edge stitch, bring threaded needle out from back to front along edge of piece.

stringing and wireworking

STRINGING

Stringing is a technique in which you use beading wire or other material to gather beads into a strand.

OPENING AND CLOSING A JUMP RING

Open a jump ring by grasping each side of its opening with a pair of pliers (chain- and/or flat-nose pliers); don't pull apart. Instead, twist in opposite directions to avoid distorting the shape. To close a jump ring, twist each side back together until the two edges meet.

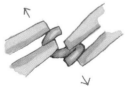

SIMPLE LOOP

To form a simple loop, use flat-nose pliers to make a 90° bend at least ½" (1.3 cm) from the end of the wire [figure 1]. Use round-nose pliers to grasp the wire after the bend; roll the pliers toward the bend, but not past it, to preserve the 90° bend. Use your thumb to continue the wrap around the nose of the pliers [figure 2]. Trim the wire next to the bend [figure 3].

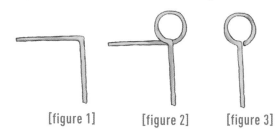

[figure 1]   [figure 2]   [figure 3]

DOUBLE SIMPLE LOOP

To form a double simple loop, make the 90° bend at least 1" (2.5 cm) from the end of the wire. Make a simple loop and continue wrapping the wire around the round-nose pliers to form two complete loops.

WRAPPED LOOP

To form a wrapped loop, use flat-nose pliers to make a 90° bend at least 2" (5 cm) from the end of the wire. Use round-nose pliers to form a simple loop with a tail overlapping the bend [figure 1]. Wrap the tail tightly down the neck of the wire to create a couple of coils. Trim the excess wire to finish [figure 2].

[figure 1]   [figure 2]

WRAPPED-LOOP LINK WITH BEAD

Create a wrapped-loop link and string a bead onto wire tail [figure 1]. Create a second wrapped-loop link on the opposite side [figures 2 and 3]. To attach wrapped-loop links, begin a wrapped loop, passing the wire tail through the previous loop before wrapping the neck of the new loop.

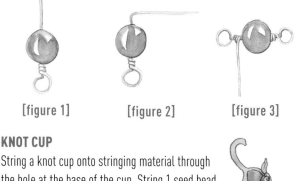

[figure 1]   [figure 2]   [figure 3]

KNOT CUP

String a knot cup onto stringing material through the hole at the base of the cup. String 1 seed bead and tie an overhand knot around the seed bead (you may want to use a drop of cement to secure the knot [figure 1]). Trim the stringing material. Use chain- or flat-nose pliers to close the cups of the knot cup around the knot. Use round-nose pliers to curl the hook down into a loop [figure 2].

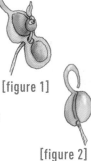

[figure 1]

[figure 2]

CRIMPING

String a crimp tube and the connection finding (i.e., the loop of a clasp). Pass back through the tube, leaving a short tail. Use the back notch of the crimping pliers to press the length of the tube down between the wires, enclosing them in separate chambers of the crescent shape [figure 1]. Rotate the tube 90° and use the front notch of the pliers to fold the two chambers onto themselves, forming a clean cylinder [figure 2]. Trim the excess wire.

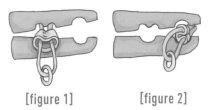

[figure 1]   [figure 2]

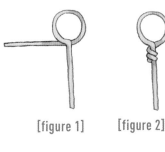

tools

A. CRIMPING PLIERS

Crimping pliers have two separate sets of grooves for molding crimp tubes to beading wire. The first set of grooves press down the length of the tube, creating two chambers. The second set pushes the two chambers together to create one cylinder.

B. ROUND-NOSE PLIERS

Round-nose pliers have smooth cone-shaped jaws for creating loops with wire.

C. CHAIN-NOSE PLIERS

Chain-nose pliers have smooth, tapered jaws for gripping wire and reaching into small spaces.

D. FLUSH OR SIDE CUTTERS

Flush or side cutters feature sharp edges for cutting wire. They are flat on one side to make smooth cuts without leaving behind sharp edges.

BALL PEEN HAMMER AND BENCH BLOCK

A ball peen hammer (not shown) and bench block (not shown) are used for hammering wire to flatten and harden shapes and add texture. Ball peen hammers are flat on one side and have a ball shape on the other. Bench blocks are often made of steel and come in several sizes.

NYLON-JAW PLIERS

Nylon-jaw pliers [not shown] have jaws that are covered with a protective coating that will not mar wire.

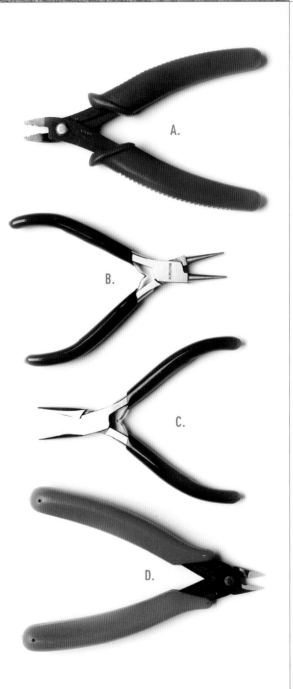

A.

B.

C.

D.

Many lovely beads and findings can be found at local bead stores, so be sure to check them out.

Ace Hardware
(866) 290-5334
acehardware.com
Natural copper wire

Artbeads.com
11901 137th Avenue Ct. KPN
Gig Harbor, WA 98329
(866) 715-BEAD (2323)
artbeads.com
Sterling silver 30-gauge wire

Artistic Wire
752 North Larch Ave.
Elmhurst, IL 60126
(630) 530-7567
artisticwire.com
Silver-plated copper wire (in silver and various colors); colored copper wire; bare copper wire

Cascade Yarns
PO Box 58168
Tukwila, WA 98138
cascadeyarns.com
Cascade 220 Wool

The Colonial Needle Company
74 Westmoreland Ave.
White Plains, NY 10606
(800) 9-NEEDLE (800-963-3353)
colonialneedle.com
Blue grip felting needles

EarthFaire
earthfaire.com
Artistic wire

Foxglove FiberArts Supply
8040 NE Day Rd., Ste 4F
Bainbridge Island, WA 98110
(206) 780-2747
foxglovefiber.com
Ashford fiber sampler bag

Habu Textiles
135 West 29th St.
Ste. 804
New York, NY 10001
(212) 239-3546
habutextiles.com
A-20 and A-21 stainless steel/silk yarn; A-148 stainless steel/wool yarn

Legendary Beads
2725 Santa Rosa Ave.
Santa Rosa, CA 95407
(707) 569-0338
legendarybeads.com
Pearl sticks; round stone beads; seed beads; coil ends

Louet.com North America
808 Commerce Park Dr.
Ogdensburg, NY 13669
14/2 Euroflax Linen; Dyed Corriedale Top

Mielke's Fiber Arts LLC
3086 Co. Rd. PP
Rudolph, WI 54475
mielkesfarm.com
Bag of candy fiber sampler bag

Out on a Whim
121 E. Cotati Ave.
Cotati, CA 94931
(800) 232-3111
whimbeads.com
Toggle clasps; chain; findings

Natural Touch Beads
Petaluma, CA
naturaltouchbeads.com
Resin beads

Rings & Things
PO Box 450
Spokane, WA 99210
(800) 366-2156
rings-things.com
Findings; silver-plated copper wire; sterling silver links; beads

Soft Flex Company
PO Box 80
Sonoma, CA 95476
(707) 938-3539
softflexcompany.com
Fine beading wire

Ubeadquitous
513 David Clayton Ln.
Windsor, CA 95492
(707) 838-3953
ubeadquitous.com
Copper findings; seed beads; Miyuki Magatamas (teardrop) beads

materials by project
WIRE

Sterling Frame Bracelet, p. 8
Artbeads.com: Sterling silver 30-gauge wire; sterling silver 16-gauge wire

Rings & Things: Faceted mixed semi-precious stone rondelles; sterling silver 5x8mm rectangular links; sterling silver 18x22mm round links; sterling silver 25mm curved bead with loop; sterling silver figure-eight connectors; sterling silver head pins

Neofiligree Necklace and Earrings , p. 16
Soft Flex: Fine beading wire

Ubeadquitous: Hammered-finish copper-plated toggle clasp; copper jump rings; copper crimp beads

Rings & Things: Faceted tigereye 10x14mm puffed rectangles

Ace Hardware: 28-gauge natural copper wire

Legendary Beads: Pearl sticks

Red in Silver Necklace, p. 22
Soft Flex: Fine beading wire

Rings & Things: 12mm round apple coral beads; apple coral 39mm "GoGo" pendant; silver-plated toggle clasp; silver-tone jump rings; silver-plated crimp beads; silver-plated 6mm cord caps; silver-plated 4mm round beads; silver-plated wire guardians

Mess-Up Necklace, p. 28
Rings & Things: Rubber cord (neoprene)

Donut Break Necklace & Earrings, p. 32
Natural Touch Beads: 32x5mm resin flat ring beads in cobalt, capri, clear, artichoke, and light blue; cobalt 31x23mm teardrop slice

Ubeadquitous: Gunmetal findings

Trio of Wire Earrings, p. 40
Earthfaire.com: 32-gauge silver-plated copper craft wire in S06 blue and S17 chartreuse

Ubeadquitous and Whimbeads.com: Findings

FIBER

Scarf Cocktail Necklace, p. 50
Habu Textiles: A-20 1/20 silk/stainless steel yarn in #3 gray

Rings & Things: Swarovski Crystals

Legendary Beads: Seed beads

Luscious Silk Bracelets, p. 56
Habu Textiles: A-20 1/20 silk/stainless steel yarn in #3 gray

Rings & Things: Silver-plated jump rings; silver-plated prong bails

Whimbeads.com: Silver-plated square pewter toggle clasp; silver-tone ear wires

Fiber Earrings, p. 64
Habu Textiles: A-21 1/20 silk/stainless steel yarn in #3 gray and #16 lavender

Whimbeads.com: Silver-tone wires; findings

In addition to the companies listed, I would like to thank Kreinik, Lanaknits Designs, Misti International, and Rowan/Westminster Fibers for generously supplying materials.

—R. H.

index

Create beautiful designs using these inspiring resources from Interweave

Hand Felted Jewelry and Beads
25 Artful Designs
Carol Huber Cypher
$21.95
ISBN 978-1-59668-005-0

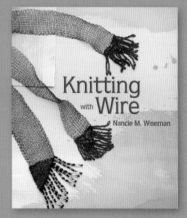

Crochet Jewelry
40 Beautiful and Unique Designs
Waejong Kim & Anna Pulvermakher
$24.95
ISBN 978-1-59668-035-7

Knitting with Wire
Nancie M. Wiseman
$16.95
ISBN 978-1-931499-31-6

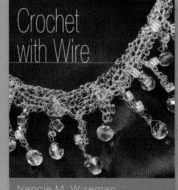

Crochet with Wire
Nancie M. Wiseman
$14.95
ISBN 978-1-931499-77-4

INTERWEAVE
interweavebooks.com